A BOY, A BIKE & BUSTER

A Boy,
A Bike
& Buster

* * * * *

*Fishing & Hunting
in Michigan's Good Old Days*

* * * * *

by **GORDON CHARLES**

ILLUSTRATIONS BY GENE HIBBARD

Gordon Charles

TRAVERSE OUTDOOR PRESS

TRAVERSE CITY, MICHIGAN

Additional copies of this book
may be ordered through bookstores
or by sending $12.95 plus $3.50
postage and handling to:
Publishers Distribution Service
6893 Sullivan Road
Grawn, MI 49637
(800) 507-2665

Publisher's Cataloging-in-Publication Data

Charles, Gordon, 1920—
A boy, a bike and Buster: fishing and hunting in Michigan's
good old days / Gordon Charles—
Traverse Outdoor Press: Traverse City, Michigan.
p. ill. cm.
ISBN: 0-9642948-0-X
1. Charles, Gordon 1920— 2. Fishers—
Michigan. 3. Hunters—Michigan—Biography.
I. Title.

SH415.C48C48	1994
799.1'092—DC20	94-61375

Printed in the United States of America
Text design by Heather Shaw Cauchy / PDS
10 9 8 7 6 5 4 3 2 1

Dedicated to my wife, Dorothy,
who married a radio announcer, then
didn't object when I later turned into a writer
which, I think, has been a lot more fun.

CONTENTS

FOREWORD

My GOOD AND longtime friend, Gordie Charles, is no one you want to take at face value.

He appears to be mild-mannered to the point of being self-effacing, quiet to the point of being barely understandable, kind to the point of being easily victimized, forgetful to the point of being absentminded.

Don't believe any of that. He is forceful when need be, loud if he has to make a point, hard as nails if someone tries to put one over on him, and his memory is detailed as an old-fashioned Sears catalogue.

That vivid detail is well illustrated in his new book, "A Boy, a Bike and Buster: Fishing and Hunting in Michigan's Good Old Days."

The book brings back to life a vanished era when it seems everybody was young, there was no crime or violence and the woods and waters were almost deserted except for us who knew their secret charms.

Gordie writes with grace about his adventures in those unspoiled woods and waters which surrounded Traverse City when he was a teenager and squeezing high school into his hunting and fishing expeditions.

I can relate to Gordie's tales, since we are close to the same age and I, too, grew up in the Depression. Maybe the big difference is that I didn't have a bicycle in high school. We were too poor to afford one. But I still managed to get my share of hunting and fishing around the northern suburbs of Detroit. I used to hunt rabbits, for example, were Northland shopping mall and its acre upon acre of parking lots now stand.

But even more than that, I, too, have my recollections of Traverse City in the 1930s. When I was in high school, my parents used to pack a secondhand army tent, some basic camping supplies, my sister and me into a battered 1928 Essex every summer and managed somehow to drive more than 200 miles north over often-gravel roads to Traverse City State Park for two weeks of camping and exploring the little backwoods town and its surroundings.

Gordie's recollections often dovetail into mine for an added delight.

But you need not be a senior citizen to enjoy Gordie's tales of days gone by. Our dear, dead days make fascinating reading even for the youngest of you out there. Read, learn and inwardly digest— and enjoy!

James A. O. Crowe
Outdoor Editor, *Detroit News*, Retired

INTRODUCTION

As a 15-YEAR-OLD living in Columbus, Ohio, in 1935, my chances of finding a life of outdoor adventure were not exactly bright. But that didn't stop me from dreaming of it most of the time.

To make up for the lack of opportunity in a big city, I became an avid reader of books dealing with strong men who dared to challenge the wilderness of Alaska and the Yukon. I, too, longed to search for gold and to grub out a living amidst hardships of every kind.

My two favorite authors were James B. Hendryx and Harold Titus. Both wrote novels in which I was able to immerse myself to such an extent that most times I read a book a day. Often I would peddle my bicycle to the local lending library and come home with a whole basket full of adventure in the far north, all of which I would eagerly devour.

How could I possibly know that by the following year I would be leaving the big city and moving to Traverse City, Michigan, with Mom, Dad and my younger sister, LaVerne. I had no idea then, either, that in the same area of Michigan lived my two idols, Jim Hendryx and Harold Titus. Both would become my friends and encourage me to become a writer, too, about the outdoors and all it contains.

Even more improbable was the fact that in the years ahead I would come to know one of the main characters in the Hendryx novels and marry his granddaughter!

Frank Hahnenberg, who was often referred to as the "Gold Tooth Kid" in some of the Hendryx novels, was a young man who lived in Lake Leelanau, just to the northwest of Traverse City. As happened to many others in 1898, when gold was discovered in the Klondike and the famous "Gold Rush" began, Hahnenberg found it impossible not to go try his luck, too.

During his days in the far north he kept careful diaries which, on his return to civilization finally, he let Jim Hendryx read. Those were the inspiration for Hendryx to turn out a whole series of his novels. They, of course, were the ones which first fired my imagination as a kid in Columbus.

In the years which followed our family move to Traverse City, I would finish high school there and become acquainted with Betty Hendryx who was in my same class, then later on, establish a friendship with her father, Jim. He was a character every bit as colorful as the ones he wrote about in his novels of the wild northland.

It was 1947, however, before I met Dorothy Hahnenberg and married her, then discovered the amazing coincidence that it was her grandfather, Frank Hahnenberg, who had provided much of the inspiration for the Jim Hendryx books I had consumed with such a passion as a city teenager. I also came to know Frank Hahnenberg as a very close friend and hunted and fished with him frequently until he finally died in his 90s.

Who, indeed, can even begin to dream of the direction in which fate will guide our lives?

In the pages which follow, however, are some of the adventures of the boy who moved "up north" in 1936. Traverse City and the surrounding area were vastly different and quiet when compared to what they have become today.

This, then, is the true story of the adventures found a half-century ago by a boy who went exploring on his bicycle in company with a little dog that showed up so unexpectedly.

A BOY, A BIKE AND BUSTER

TRAVERSE CITY IN 1936

IT WAS A typical December day in 1936 when the train pulled into the station at Traverse City, Michigan. As Dad looked out the coach window and saw snow banks piled to amazing heights and more of the white stuff blowing in off frozen Boardman Lake, he had second thoughts.

"I very nearly stayed right on board to go back to Columbus," he told us later.

Fortunately, he didn't. Instead, he reluctantly climbed off, collected his suitcase, then was met by Charlie Garthe who had a car and took him home with him. Charlie and his brother, Lud Garthe, were the main owners of the Grand Traverse Metal Casket Company and, in that year, they needed the help of a good mold maker to turn out the ornamental trimmings on their famous product.

Dad, whose name was Edward P. Zimmerman, was-my step-father, who had married my mother, Myrtle, when my sister, LaVerne, and I were still quite young. Neither of us ever thought of Dad as anything but our own father and that feeling was mutual with all of us.

The Garthes knew they had a real find when they hired Dad, even if they did have to pay him $40 a week. At the time, his was one of the best salaries, especially in Traverse City. Dad had worked for years at Michael's Art Bronze in Cincinnati and some of his resulting works are still on useful display in Washington, D.C. on the Lincoln Memorial and several other federal buildings.

Following the market crash of 1929, however, a lot of business places went bankrupt. Among them was the one where Dad had worked. Most of the 1930s to follow were known as years of the "Great Depression" and work of any kind was nearly impossible to find.

For a time, we survived by moving in with my mother's Aunt Rose Helmes who lived on Darwin Avenue out in Cheviot, then a Cincinnati suburb. In the meantime, Dad scrounged up every bit of work he could find, including a stint at digging ditches with the old WPA or Works Project Administration. From there, he had a chance to take us all to Columbus where he had one of the dirtiest jobs imaginable — cleaning coal furnaces. He always came back home utterly black from top to bottom and Mom worried about his health from breathing in such crud. Dad was determined, though, and kept looking for something better but it was three years before the Traverse City offer came along.

During the time we lived in Columbus, I helped out as best I could, too. Lawn mowing was my big money project and my best customer was a lady who lived over in the Grandview area. Her lawn covered nearly a half-acre and I did the whole thing with a hand-pushed mower. It took nearly all day but she paid me 50 cents and midway of the job she always rewarded me with a glass of milk and a cookie. I considered it all a great deal.

From there, I went on to bigger things. The "Columbus Dispatch" was advertising for a new carrier in our area and asked for written applications from interested boys. I took pen in hand and dashed off a note, saying that although I didn't have a bicycle just yet, I was "a real fast walker."

I got the job and before long had earned enough money that

I was able to take a bus downtown to Lazarus Department Store. There I bought the bicycle of my dreams and rode it home from the heart of the city. I felt like I was really king of the world!

It was a magnificent bicycle with balloon tires and had one unique feature. By turning the front wheel hard to the left, a key could be taken out and the bike was left locked in that position, thus making it impossible to steal and ride away. I later bought a big wire basket for the handlebars so I could carry extra newspapers as well as library books and, of course, my school books.

When Dad went to Traverse City he roomed with the Henry Houdek family on West Eighth Street for a couple of weeks. He was then able to finally locate a house to rent, although he was rather shocked about paying $25 a month, which he considered quite high. The house was owned by Otto Kyselka and was located on East Ninth Street, just off South Union Street in what is still called "Old Town" in Traverse City. The location was great, since it was only two blocks from the casket company where Dad worked.

To save as much money as possible, the Garthes agreed to let Dad accompany Archie Dennis when they took one of the company trucks to Columbus to pick up our furniture. I was allowed to ride along, too, on the return trip when we also took along our female German shepherd dog, "Tex," as well as my beloved bicycle which I personally put on the truck.

Mom and LaVerne had to head north on the train, which I considered a less exciting way to travel, even if they did get to Traverse City almost as soon as we did.

Our new home had two bedrooms downstairs while the upstairs consisted of one room big enough that it could have been divided. Mom and Dad said I could have that one and I was delighted to have so much space, even if the walls did slope, due to being just under the roof. It didn't take long for

3

me to create my own sort of museum up there, decorating it with all sorts of rocks, shells, pinecones and other outdoor treasures. There were even a few bird nests, carefully hidden, so my mother would overlook them.

The house also had a full basement which could be reached by an indoor stairway or, better yet, through a pair of doors outside. That, Dad and I figured, would make it possible for us to build some special projects indoors. The first was to be a fish shanty to go on Boardman Lake's ice where Dad had a full view from his workshop window at the casket company. I also decided it could be ideal for building some sort of boat for warm weather, should I ever be able to get that much money together.

The fact that we had no car, much less a trailer to transport such objects, didn't bother us since we were sure something could be figured out when the right time came. Even the thought of a car was impossible because the folks still had debts to pay off and, besides we could walk to nearly anywhere in Traverse City we wanted to go. As for longer distances, Dad and I could double up on my bicycle if we really wanted to go anywhere special, we decided.

Dad had to laugh at one joke on himself. During the first week he had spent in Traverse City he figured that the two-block-long stretch of South Union Street he saw was all there was to the town. He wrote and told us so in Columbus, saying Nesbitt's had a pretty nice hardware store and there was a Wahl's drugstore with a fine soda fountain. In addition, there was Zobel's Dairy just around the corner from where we finally ended up living and Fred Birdsey's barbershop, also close by.

His next letter quickly followed, saying he was wrong and there was "a lot more to Traverse City than I first thought." He had walked on north and discovered the real downtown area. That', he said, included the five-story Traverse Hotel plus an even taller structure, the Park Place Hotel. There were all kinds of stores, including the huge Hannah & Lay building on Front Street and even a pool hall called Conaway's.

Traverse City, he predicted, was going to be a fine place to live.

Dad was right.

Action was almost guaranteed when fishing for
pike on Boardman lake,

EXCITING ICE FISHING

GOING ICE FISHING in a casket box might not appeal to today's younger generation. But, back in the winter of 1936-37, it turned out to be plenty of fun for several of us.

Our family hadn't been in Traverse City very long before learning that ice fishing was one of the big winter pastimes, partly because it was cheap. On a good day you might be able to add something substantial to the home menu at little or no cost. That was pretty important in those days of necessary dollar-stretching.

With Dad working at the casket company, he and I figured out an economical way to create our own fish shanty, too. Among those working with him were Ivan and Esther Swaney who fitted in the fancy linings of the metal caskets. The material came in big boxes that were made of thin veneer and were of near-perfect fish shanty size.

That's how Dad and I came to be sliding one of the big boxes down the East Ninth Street sidewalk on the snow one day to where we lived. It fit through the outer doors leading down into the basement, a perfect place for us to do our work on it.

We stood it on end in order to have ample headroom, cut a couple holes in what was to be the floor, then built a door so we could get in and out easily. With that done, we then rigged up a little wood stove, using an old metal pail and ran some small stovepipe up and through the roof, being sure it was kept away from the wood by a metal flange. In all, it looked like a great little building.

Not having a car, we had to slide our new shanty, on makeshift runners, to Boardman Lake, three blocks away. We had heard it was a good northern pike lake. It was. And still is.

Weekdays, as soon as school was over, I always headed for the shanty and spent nearly-every Saturday there, too. Generally, I could figure that it wouldn't be long, either, before there was a pounding on the shanty door.

That was usually Fred Swaney. He was Ivan and Esther's son and I considered him a pesky little kid. He was two years younger than I was but sort of made up for that with his enthusiasm for anything outdoors, a trait with which I could easily relate.

Fred's major talent seemed to be in entertaining local groups with a program of "snappy tap dancing," as it was advertised in the Traverse City Record-Eagle. Despite that, his personality overcame my reluctance to associate with him and we became great friends, a condition that still exists today, a half-century later.

Most of what we caught through the shanty floor and from ice holes some distance away, were pike barely over the legal 14 inches then in effect. Still, when we got one in the 20-inch class, it really looked like a whopper. We pretty much kept everything we pulled from beneath the ice, partly to help feed our families but probably mostly to feed our ego as proof of what mighty fishermen we really were.

Not having the money to buy commercial tip-ups, we froze long, willow wands into the ice so they hung over the fishing hole. The line had a loop tied in it and this was slipped over the stick so when a pike hit, the willow would twitch and bend. A big pike would just rip the line off the stick and run with the minnow bait so it called for some careful watching as we didn't want to risk losing any of our lines.

Ultimately, we fashioned our own tip-ups, complete with underwater reels that didn't freeze up on real cold days. The best reels we made were created from two small, metal pie tins soldered back to back. It was a lot of fun watching our own creations perform just as well as store variety tip-ups.

While Boardman Lake was okay as a fishing hole, it was really only a make-shift arrangement until Grand Traverse Bay froze out in front of Traverse City. In 1937 that happened on February 21 and shortly afterwards Dad and I hand-pushed our casket box close to a mile to a site we had earlier picked out near the old We-Que-Tong Club.

Used as a yacht club by the local society set, it was also popular with the younger folks in summer as a dance spot. I couldn't have cared less about such back then but within a year or two in high school I discovered that holding a sweet young thing in your arms on a dance floor was darned near as interesting as watching for a tip-up flag to pop.

Nobody knew back then that the old We-Que-Tong was on borrowed time. Eventually, it was torn down to make way for the new Grandview Parkway which skirts the bay. That called for shifting the Boardman River mouth which now flows very close to where the ornate old building once sat.

Copying techniques of nearby fishermen soon had Dad and me in business catching yellow perch and lake herring which everybody called ciscoes. Both liked tiny minnows but ciscoes preferred pearl button lures even more.

Shirts back then had those genuine buttons but they had to be ground down very thin to give them a little bit of a concave shape. That brought out the real pearl glow and an enticing action that ciscoes found hard to resist when fluttering through the water in a jigging motion. (Mom must have wondered why my shirts lacked so many buttons.)

Most of our ciscoes ranged from ten inches to twice that long but they all had to be handled gingerly. Tiny mouths were very tender and a big one had to be grasped before lifting it from the water to prevent tearing loose.

Ciscoes also run in schools and when one was caught, others were usually close by. To keep them around, we often shucked some of the soft, sparkling cisco scales down the shanty holes, creating the illusion of a school of minnows. When we lacked a cisco in the shanty, we substituted a small handful of eggshells which we first crushed before spilling them down the ice hole. They pretty much served the same purpose.

Perch preferred little minnows, a strip of belly from another perch or a perch eye but we sometimes caught them on the pearl buttons, too. Most ran seven or eight inches long, perfect for the pan and unbeatable in flavor. All were welcome in our menus.

During the week, Dad's working hours prevented him from getting in as much fishing time as I could manage since I had extra daylight after school. I also took note of the fact that some fishermen were doing better than we had so I decided to move the shanty to a better location, too.

Since Fred Swaney could always be prevailed upon to help, he and I hurried to the bay one noontime to relocate the casket box fish shanty. It had a pair of old skis for runners and pulled rather easily but on that day there was something of a head wind. Accordingly, I had Fred pull on the rope ahead while I pushed from the rear.

While that seemed like a logical arrangement, I hadn't counted on Fred's scatterbrained attitude. Figuring a straight line was the shortest distance between two points, he followed a route that took us right over a spot where another shanty had been located a short time before.

Coming to it, Fred stepped over the spearing hole but, unable to see it and with no warning from him, went right into the water up to my waist, good school clothes and all.

"Oh, didn't you see that hole?" Fred said with his usual wide-eyed display of innocence, ignoring the fact that there was no way I could see through the shanty I was pushing.

My reply to him right then is best left unrepeated! That was one day I had an unexcused absence from school because, obviously, I couldn't be expected to go to classes in my soggy condition. Besides, my teeth were chattering from the un-planned dip in Grand Traverse Bay.

Mom and Dad, though, insisted that Sunday was always for church. I grumbled somewhat but went along with them and LaVerne to Central Methodist Church on South Cass Street. From the top steps it was possible to see the bay, though, and one Sunday as we came out I noticed the ice out there doing strange things. I convinced Dad that we should walk over to check on our shanty.

While the bay was still-frozen, an extremely strong north wind was blowing toward Traverse City. Far up the bay, the ice had broken up and waves were actually rolling under the remaining ice coating. Oddly, it had not yet broken up at the south end but was bending and groaning under the unusual stresses being exerted against it.

It was obvious the bay was about to break up. As we stood there glumly watching, a lad came by." I'll go out and get your shanty for a dollar," he offered. Dad declined, saying he wouldn't risk anyone's life like that for any price.

Sadly, we watched as one after another of the cluster of shanties tipped and fell into open water that soon appeared as the ice gradually gave way. Not wanting to see our beloved casket box meet a similar fate, we turned and walked on home.

Next day, I just had to get back there to see if anything could be seen of our little fishing structure. I was shocked and delighted to find it still sitting jauntily on the ice that was, once again, firmly joined together by an unusually low temperature during the night.

When Dad got home from work, the two of us walked out to get our shanty. We found we had, unknowingly, put it on one of the thickest pieces of drift ice in the bay and that is what saved it.

Dad, however, had other-ideas to explain the salvation of our beloved fish shanty. "See what happens when you go to church on Sundays?" he commented.

Buster had fun chasing cottontails through the
big pipes stacked at old Traverse City Iron Works.

BUSTER THE BEAGLE

WHAT RED-BLOODED MALE could possibly resist the charms of a beautiful, long-legged redhead? Buster certainly couldn't. It was obvious, just by looking at him, to tell he was in love. But, as fate too often wills it, the object of his affections did not feel likewise. She barely tolerated him.

None of us even knew the little beagle's name when he first came calling on our unusual-colored, red German shepherd. Our whole family agreed it would be pretty much of a mismatch anyhow and were happy that Tex felt that way, too.

It was springtime in 1937, a time of year when all dogs tend to go wandering, given the opportunity. Our new Traverse City home had a gravel alley running alongside it and it was on this route that Buster made his rounds, obviously seeking romance. We couldn't really tell which direction from us he might live because he showed up from a variety of points and left, grudgingly, the same way.

None of us did anything to encourage him, at least not at first. Although Tex was only two-thirds the size of a normal German shepherd. she still towered over the tiny beagle who stood only 11.5 inches tall at the shoulder. He looked like a full-line, registered beagle except for his ears which were not much longer than those of a fox terrier.

We had acquired Tex during the three years we lived in Columbus during the struggling days of the Great Depression. When first moving there from Cincinnati to a new job that didn't last, Dad promised to get a dog for LaVerne and me. He came home one day with a cute little German shepherd puppy which we promptly named "Rex" because we were so sure he was going to grow up to become a king of canines as great as the famous Rin-Tin-Tin of movie fame.

It didn't work out that way, though. Pet shops in those days were not as careful about puppy shots and within a matter of weeks it became evident that Rex had distemper in its final stages. Despite everything we could do, he finally died.

Watching that happen to an innocent puppy can tear your heart apart and when it ended all of us cried without shame. We felt we had lost a family member, which, in fact, we had.

Less than a year later, an oddly-colored dog, ribs showing plainly through her red hair, showed up at our house and tried to scavenge in the garbage can out back. Feeling sorry for her, we fed her some of Rex's leftover dog chow.

It wasn't our intention to adopt her but that's the way it finally turned out. She refused to leave our yard. Even more-amazing to us, whenever some questionable character would come wandering down the alley she would drive him away from our place.

Inquiring around the neighborhood and watching the want ads in the Columbus Dispatch did no good. Nobody, apparently, wanted this dog and had abandoned her, possibly because she was just another mouth to feed in those hard times.

That she had adopted us became quite apparent but we didn't object too much as she filled a void we had all been feeling. Perhaps it was only natural that, as successor to Rex, she would be called Tex. We made sure she was on the moving van when we headed north from Ohio to northern Michigan during the previous winter.

Knowing how easy it is to impress a stray dog with food, though, we went out of our way to avoid feeding Buster when he showed up on our doorstep. However, Tex must have come to enjoy his company somewhat and began to leave a little something to eat in her food dish which the little beagle eagerly cleaned up. How do you combat something like that?

Again, we tried to locate the owner of a stray dog. We asked over on South Union Street at Zobel's Dairy and at Fred Birdsey's barbershop, meanwhile watching the Record-Eagle want ads. Nobody, it seemed, was missing a little lop-eared beagle.

Eventually, Buster wheedled his way into our hearts and home, becoming another family member. We found he was also an entertainer and could sit up on his hind legs and beg. If that failed to win him a snack, he would drop back down, spin around in a tight circle and roll over before popping back up into a sitting position again.

To be fair about it all, though, we frequently let him out of the house, feeling there was still the chance he would go back to wherever his original home might be and a real owner might be waiting for him. secretly, we all hoped that would never happen.

But it did. He was gone two days and a night before finally showing up at our house again for a joyful reunion with the four of us and Tex. Next morning, however, he wanted to go out so Dad and I turned him loose but followed him north up the alley as he trotted purposefully along.

We were fearful of what might happen as we passed in the alley behind Wilhelm's, then Nesbitt's hardware store and finally approached Seventh Street. There, Buster turned toward the old Park Hotel (it later became Bun Brady's Bar) and went up to the back door.

A few minutes later, in response to the dog's insistent

scratching on the door, a stocky man dressed in a dirty white apron came out and reached down to pet Buster. It was painfully obvious to us, in the greeting the dog gave back that this was really his master. I got a sick feeling in my stomach and, looking at Dad, knew he felt the same way.

Even so, we went up to talk to the man who, it turned out, was cook at the little hotel. Dad explained that we had taken in the dog to feed him and give him a home until we could find the rightful owner. The cook said he really appreciated that since he had been called out of town for more than two months and had been unable to find Buster (that's the first we knew his real name) before he left.

Despite his small size and shortage of long ears, Buster was actually a registered beagle. He had once been owned by Austin Batdorff, the owner of the Traverse City Record-Eagle, who gave him to the Park Hotel cook. (Little did I then dream that one day I would work for the Batdorffs as outdoor editor of the newspaper.)

Thanking us for our kindness to his dog, the cook went back inside, taking Buster with him. Dad and I trudged back down the alley toward home feeling terrible, yet still thankful that we had helped a little dog find his way back to his real owner.

A week went by, then the cook showed up at our door with Buster under one arm. "I've decided to take a job in Florida and won't be able to take Buster along with me," he said. Would you like to have him to keep for your own dog?"

Boy, would we! The cook (we never did get his name) did nothing to-allay our enthusiasm when he mentioned that the little beagle was also an excellent rabbit dog. "He goes over across Seventh Street to the Traverse City Iron Works and does his practicing there'll he explained.

Several weeks later, my curiosity got the best of me and I took Buster down to the Iron Works to see if it was true. It was. The little dog immediately began to poke his wet, black nose in among the massive heaps of big cast-iron pipes that were stacked between Seventh Street and the Union Street Dam.

In minutes he had a cottontail rabbit going and ran it relentlessly in and out of the pipes with the prettiest chorus of beagle music I have ever heard. The sound was amplified by the inner pipe areas in much the same manner as a pipe organ, although the tune was obviously quite different. At no point, of course, were any of those wild rabbits in danger of being caught. I figured they enjoyed being pursued just as much as Buster did chasing them.

(Many years later, the Iron Works moved to a new location, taking along its stock of big iron pipes. In time, the old buildings deteriorated to such an extent that in 1989, new owners of the property were forced to tear them down to make way for another use.)

When I arrived back home with Buster and reported what he could do with the Iron Works bunnies, Dad reminded me that Michigan's rabbit hunting season would soon be starting. "We better get some guns," he said. I, of course, didn't need any further urging. I was about to purchase my first real shotgun.

Fred Birdsey's barbershop was the logical place to start looking. In addition to rolling up profits of 25 cents for each haircut, Fred kept an impressive rack of used guns in a corner of his shop which adjoined the Birdsey living quarters.

To a teenage boy, it looked like an impossible task to select the one perfect shotgun from all of the automatics, pumps, doubles and single-shots. Dad, however, steered me away from the complicated scatterguns and suggested one of the singles would be best for just starting out. "You'll learn to shoot a lot better with a single, knowing you only have one shot," he wisely counciled.

I found out later how true that was. A guy just doesn't take chances by wasting a shell on an "iffy" shot when he might

19

hold up briefly and maybe get a better chance.

My selection was finally a single-shot 16-gauge that came up to my shoulder perfectly and pointed exactly where I was looking, all in the same motion. I winced, though, at the $5 price, and wondered how I could ever possibly be able to afford that much in addition to the shotgun shells which were nearly $1 a box.

Finally digging into the meager amount of money I had managed to save up from a summer job, I paid for my first shotgun. The remainder of my summer earnings had already been spent on clothes for school, so shells could be a problem.

That was finally solved when I went to my mother and struck a deal with her. She agreed to pay me 25 cents apiece for each rabbit or similar-sized game animal or bird and ten cents for each squirrel or its equivalent amount of meat. That, she said, would not only help keep me supplied with the cash to buy shells but would be a fine contribution in keeping the family supplied with an extra source of food.

I was elated. With the aid of Buster the beagle, I was about to become a "market hunter" of sorts in the great north woods of Michigan!

Pedaling away to hunting adventure with Buster
in the bike basket usually led to a lot of fun.

BICYCLE HUNTING

A T THE INSISTENCE of most sportsmen, hunting sea
sons in the late 1930s were of short duration. Duck
hunting always began October 1 but seasons on
rabbits, pheasants, grouse and such didn't start until October
15.

Bird hunting closed down again November 14 to make way
for the big deer hunt, even though not all parts of Michigan
were open for whitetails, Leelanau County, for example, was
among the last in the state to allow deer hunting.

It was in the fall of 1937 when I first sallied forth with my
brand new, second-hand, 16-gauge shotgun. I was a high
school junior by then and considered such education pretty
much of a nuisance. After all, how could a guy do any amount
of hunting if he had to confine it to just weekends?

Mom and Dad, though, insisted I had to finish high school
so I set about trying to figure out some logical way of doing a
little weekday hunting, too. My solution, applied today, would
give teachers and everybody else fits. But back then nobody
thought a thing of my method.

I took my shotgun to school with me. It was in a cloth case
Mom had sewn for me and I kept it in my locker on the lower
floor of the building on West Eighth Street which was then
Traverse City High School. (It later became a grade school

23

when a new high school was built in a more central location.)

Since we were still struggling out of the effects of the Great Depression, owning a car was unthinkable, much less driving one to school then. My transportation was a shiny, balloon-tired bicycle that was parked just outside the Seventh Street door. Nobody bothered to lock a bike then. We just didn't have any crime. My bike, though, had a unique lock that was controlled by a sort of ignition key which left it locked when it was removed. Without the key, the bike could only go in tight circles.

My hunting plan called for split-second timing. Or almost. The final school bell of the day always rang at 3:45 p.m. Legal shooting time for ducks ended at 4:00 p.m. sharp. The closest place I might find these elusive waterfowl was on Skeet Club Point, so-called because that is where some of the wealthy Traverse City menfolk used to shoot clay pigeons. That sport, of course, was far out of my meager financial means. Besides, they weren't edible.

The point was located on the west shore of Boardman Lake, about two miles from the high school building. with only 15 minutes available, there was no time at all to be wasted.

At the first ping of the dismissal bell, I was out of my desk seat, heading downstairs two at a time. The cased shotgun came out of my locker in the same motion as the books were tossed in.

Two short straps buckled the gun crosswise to my bicycle handlebars and I began pedaling like mad toward Boardman Lake. I was proudest of the day I made it with five minutes to spare. That was the time I found a big raft of bluebill ducks sitting almost on the point and I was able to sneak down the bank behind some brush before they saw me.

With just a single-shot scattergun, I was lucky to knock down one of the big male scaup. It fell far out in the lake but a sympathetic breeze finally drifted it right back to my feet.

Hail the mighty hunter!

That same point later yielded several bufflehead ducks to my marksmanship, although there were also periodic misses that I was reluctant to discuss with anyone.

It was with something of a shock when I later saw the entire Traverse City Skeet Club torn down and the area was abandoned until a variety of industrial buildings were erected there. Among them today is a part of Northwestern Michigan College, a facility that back then wasn't even a dream. Today, that entire south end of Boardman Lake is also off-limits to hunting.

My faithful bicycle carried me on other waterfowl hunting trips around the area, too, but mostly on weekends or holidays when school could not interfere.

There was the day, for example, when I was hunting the reed beds that then swayed in thick profusion along much of the shoreline of West Grand Traverse Bay's western shore. I was wading in my hip boots and surprised a pair of huge mallards, dropping both with a single shot. They weighed 4.5 pounds apiece when I got them back home.

Several days later, I read on Ebb Warren's outdoor page in the Record-Eagle about another hunter from downstate who blasted nine mallards not far from the same spot. Only thing, he found out the hard way that they belonged to the lady who ran Smith's Fish Market, close by. He finally paid her a dollar apiece for them. It got me to wondering about the two big greenheads I had bagged but I never did go to Smith's to find out for sure.

One of my favorite spots for ducks was in a tiny, rush-filled pond that could not be seen in its entirety from what later became highway M-22 in Leelanau County. I found that I could sneak down there, through the brush, and nearly always surprise a flock of mallards or black ducks.

Some years later, I was horrified to find a drag-line working there to enlarge the pond and connect it with the remainder of the bay. Eventually, it became the present site of Harbor West, a plush marina with many millions of dollars worth of cruisers, trolling and sailboats tied up there. Nearby are stacks of fairly new condominiums and the massive Lake States Insurance building.

Today, it is difficult to remember when the shores of both bays were not ringed with houses and business places. In 1937, it seemed as though this would always remain in a semi-wilderness state.

One day, shortly after I found a bargain on shotgun shells at Trude Hardware, I bought two boxes from Clyde Wilson for a total of $1.85 and decided to splurge a few shots on elusive jacksnipe.

Those shorebirds were extremely plentiful then in many areas around both arms of Grand Traverse Bay. A spot I could always count on, after pedaling my bicycle out there, was along the corner of East Bay near where the Traverse Bay Blanket Company now sits. It was a solid mass of rushes and reeds which, combined with shallow water, was a paradise for the long-billed snipe.

It was necessary to don hip boots to keep dry, then wade slowly through the water plants in order to approach the hidden birds. Even so, I was never quite prepared when one could spring into the air and go wheeling away with its familiar "scaip, scaip, scaip" cry. often there might be a half-dozen or more in the air at one time, thus adding to the confusion.

Smaller than a woodcock, they flew with all of the accuracy of a corkscrew, particularly on days of high winds. Even today, I still have trouble hitting the little rascals which remain one of the top challenges of bird hunting.

Most of that East Bay reed bed disappeared when state engineers sucked sand out of the bay and pumped it ashore to build the present US-31 between Traverse City and Acme.

Business places completed the disaster by filling in what few rush beds remained between the highway and the uplands. With these low bog holes gone so were the jacksnipe as well as ducks and a number of other birds.

Bob Fifarek, one of my classmates, came close to matching my enthusiasm for this kind of hunting. His father, however, owned a car and Bob was able to get him to drive him up north to Lee's Point, near where my idol, Jim Hendryx, lived. Bob and his beagle would be dropped off there to run rabbits for about an hour, then they would begin to hunt back in the direction of Traverse city, collecting ducks and jacksnipe as they went. "Dad always picked me up before I walked all the way back," Bob said.

Black ducks remained a favorite gamebird but they were so wary they were hard to find and even more difficult to approach without them flushing wild. one place I liked to hunt nearly always had blacks. It was a little pothole near the headwaters of Mitchell Creek.

I had to hike in to a little patch of hardwoods that always seemed to be partly flooded. The blacks hated to leave its near-perfect protection and I always wore hip boots so as to wade in after them as quietly and carefully as possible. Even so, they always seemed to hear me before I was quite ready and seemed to jump straight up off the water, beating their wings to carry them to treetop height before leveling out and twisting away in flight.

That never failed to startle me but it was usually possible to recover long enough to drop at least one duck and sometimes slam another shell into the single-shot in time to get a second swing on another late-jumping black.

One time when I had scored such a double, I was able to find just one black duck. Search though I might, the second duck remained hidden among the stumps and other downed timber scattered through the woodland pothole. After looking well over an hour, I decided I couldn't do the job alone, even if I wouldn't admit defeat.

Hiking back out to where my bicycle was located, I jumped on and pedaled back home. There I picked up my little beagle buddy, Buster, poked him into a knapsack with just his head sticking out and tied him in securely. With him riding in the bike basket, I pedaled back to the Mitchell Creek area, slipped my hip boots back on and we headed for the pothole area.

For all of the effort expended, it hardly seemed fair but results were so fast I couldn't believe it. Buster went splashing in through the shallow water, probably thinking it was a stupid place to look for a rabbit. In a matter of minutes, he stopped, tail wagging furiously as he peered under a stump.

I looked under it and, sure enough, there was my black duck trying to hide in water too shallow to submerge completely. I reached in and grabbed it with one hand and gave Buster an enthusiastic, thumping pat on the rear with the other hand.

Recently, I went back to the same place out of curiosity, mostly to see if the area had changed much. It was pretty discouraging. East Bay Township, along with much of the area surrounding Traverse City, has undergone vast, nearly unbelievable changes. From the standpoint of a hunter, they have not been for the best.

In about the same place where Buster found the black duck for me, there is a growing subdivision. The house that sits in the spot that was once a permanent pothole, is on ground that has been drained somehow and filled. I would be willing to bet, though, that somebody has water in the basement every once in a while and wonders why.

The same holds true of many homes built around the shores of Grand Traverse Day. That vast, beautiful body of water fluctuates periodically, according to nature's whims. Developers, however, have blissfully ignored that and have sold homes built on such low levels that when the bays rise to normal levels the buildings are subject to flooding.

In earlier days, higher ground was the preferred place to build but as the Grand Traverse Region is subjected to increasing populations, good frontage is becoming scarce and new building goes on in some pretty stupid places.

Too many smelt in the homemade onion sack net
caused the bottom to tear out.

SMELT WERE SURE FUN

A S A KID in Ohio, I didn't have the foggiest idea of what a smelt might be. Once our family had moved to Traverse City, however, all of that changed. In fact, smelt dipping was a true rite of spring, even though it all came about purely by accident.

There is an interesting saying, in fact, which undergoes testing every spring in northern Michigan. It goes something like this: "When water temperatures reach 42 degrees, the streams turn silver."

While this might baffle some individuals, it makes plenty of sense to outdoor folks. It means that smelt runs really get underway in earnest when the water temperatures hit 42 degrees. And, these silvery little fish run in such heavy numbers that creeks and even rivers sometimes seem to turn to silver.

Nobody really planned all of this. It seems that some member of the old Michigan Fish Commission obtained smelt eggs from Green Lake, Maine in 1912. They were hatched and planted in Benzie County's Crystal Lake as a new food source for landlocked salmon which went into that lake at the same time.

The landlocks promptly vanished without a trace and just

about everyone forgot the project. But in 1918, a fellow named Newt Ely of Beulah walked down to Cold Creek, which flowed alongside his house. He dipped out a couple buckets of water so his wife could do the laundry, which is how they did things in those days.

Imagine Newt's surprise to hear a splashing in the pails. He looked down and found he had a bunch of lively, silvery little fish in them. He thus became Michigan's first smelt dipper!

During the years that followed, Cold Creek and Crystal Lake became nationally famous for fun in the springtime. Smelt dippers converged on the little stream in such fantastic numbers that dipping schedules had to be set up. Upwards of 20,000 men, women and children were known to have dipped more than a ton of smelt each day for 11 days one spring.

By the time the spring of 1937 was rolling around, I was hearing all about smelt dipping and the fame of Cold Creek, too, so I determined to do something about it, even lacking any real way to get from Traverse City to the Beulah area.

Scrounging around at a couple of grocery stores, I found several mesh bags that had once contained onions. Somewhere else, I dug up a fairly heavy piece of rounded iron and bent it into a hoop which I then wrapped onto a length of old broomstick. By opening up the onion sacks and sewing them together again, I was able to come up with a smelt net that looked pretty good to a teenaged kid.

Dad thought it was pretty ingenious, too. Anyhow, when he went to work the next day he mentioned it to a young fellow who also worked with him at the Grand Traverse Metal Casket Company. This guy, named Gerald "Buck" Williams, thought it might be a good idea to try out my new net.

He volunteered to take it to Crystal Lake on a school night, which is why I wasn't allowed to go along. He would, he promised, report back to Dad next day to let us know how it worked.

The "report" turned out to be quite a steamy one. It went something like this:

Gerald (which is what Dad always called him) drove over to Beulah right after work so as to be able to get a good position when the smelt dipping was due to begin. In fact, he was able to get right in the front row of the crowd gathered behind the rope barrier which held the eager dippers back.

By then it was quite dark but the rules called for the crowd to remain where they were for some time in order to allow plenty of smelt to enter the creek on their spawning run. Finally, at the magic moment, the strings of lights over the creek were turned on, the barrier rope was dropped and the howling mob of dippers surged into Cold Creek.

Since he was in front, Gerald had the best chance. He rushed into the water, dipped my net in and made a scoop all the way to the other side. The mesh was filled nearly to bursting with hundreds of silvery, wriggling little fish.

But, when he attempted to raise the weight from the creek, my carefully constructed smelt net gave way. The bottom of it opened and every fish in it spilled back into the water!

Back at work the next morning, Gerald was still turning the air slightly blue as he explained to Dad that anybody should have known better than to make a smelt net out of paper onion sacks. Naturally, when the mesh came into contact with the water, the paper softened and the net just plain came apart.

Well, time does tend to heal and a little later on, after things had cooled down, Gerald and I got together and decided it was something of a draw. He lost the smelt but I, after all, had also lost a net. We got to be such good friends that I got to calling him "Buck" just like nearly everybody else did.

Buck Williams, of course, finally left the Casket Company to go to work for the City of Traverse City and eventually retired from one of the top positions. He went on from there to become a city commissioner.

Although Buck managed to get in on other, later smelt dips at Beulah (he bought his own net after that classic fumble) he never did duplicate the huge bagfull of fish he had the night the net broke.

Eventually, somebody in the old Conservation Department also decided that Cold Creek should be closed to smelt dipping. It was thought that the little fish were too valuable to be taken that way and it would deplete the lake's famous winter smelt fishery. Thus was lost the favorite spring pastime of many people in northern Michigan, although less spectacular dips are still held by lantern light on other streams each spring.

It has since been proved that most of Crystal Lake's smelt spawn in the rocky shoreline shallows, rather than in Cold Creek but the order closing it has never been rescinded. Conservation officers are still arresting the few who just can't resist sneaking in for a net full of smelt which had, for so long, been legal to take that way.

Smelt put into Crystal Lake in 1912, of course, didn't all stay there. Many went over the outlet dam and into Lake Michigan before spreading to all of the other Great Lakes. They surge up countless creeks and rivers in the springtime whenever water temperatures say the time is right. And, dippers still have a great time pursuing this nightly fun.

Crystal Lake still retains its winter smelt fishery. Fishing shanties dot its ice, particularly right out in front of Beulah near where Cold Creek flows in. Some of the fishing structures are really like small palaces and have all the comforts of home, including television sets, cooking stoves and even bunks for those times when the fishing might be rather slow.

Since smelt are such prolific little fish, it is understandable that Crystal Lake's winter fishery and the dipping in Cold Creek did not remain an exclusive. For a number of years, Boyne City had its own "Smeltania," during which fish shanties sprang up on the ice of Lake Charlevoix like mush-rooms. Why that fishery finally vanished, is a good question.

Suttons Bay and Bowers Harbor in the Traverse City area still have winter smelt fishing but neither has come close to approaching the fame of either Crystal Lake or the Boyne area.

When it comes to spring smelt -dipping, though, the streams of Michigan still produce plenty of action, mostly at night. Among the best in the Grand Traverse region are at Leland in the river, as well as the lower Platte River and from the piers at Frankfort and Elberta. None of those sites have "organized dipping," although they could have. Instead, the runs are often deflected by too many eager dip-netters wading out as far as possible into Lake Michigan to meet any suspected schools of smelt. That often frightens the smelt and they head back out to deeper waters until most of the dippers get tired and go back home.

In some spots, the best of the dipping is done with throw nets. These are square shape in a sort of umbrella design. The net is tossed out, sometimes from the end of a long pole, and left submerged until smelt begin to swim over the top of the mesh. The net is then quickly pulled up and, if lucky, there are a bunch of wriggling, silvery smelt to be plucked out and added to a pail containing others. The Front Street Bridge is also sometimes popular for this purpose when smelt runs come up the Boardman River.

In most rivers and creeks, tributary to the Great Lakes, the Department of Natural Resources allows smelt dipping as far as a half-mile upstream. Supposedly, though, dippers are required to not try to scoop out steelhead trout, many of which are also making spawning runs upstream then.

One night on Mitchell Creek, when lanterns and flashlights were flitting up and down the stream, I overheard something which made me smile. A father and son were obviously hoping to bring home a good mess of smelt and were quietly wading in the lower creek, away from other dippers doing the same thing.

Suddenly, there was a tremendous splashing, then a brief silence. It was broken by the kid's excited yell, "Wow, Dad, that's really a big one!"

His father's reply was somewhat subdued but still clear as he cautioned: "Shut up, kid!"

"Nice fish you've got there, young man," said
Mark Craw, the local game warden.

TROUT METHODS VARIED

Opening day of trout season in northern Michigan was always a big event in the 1930s. That, at least, remains pretty much the same even though some of it has undergone changes, too.

As a teenager in 1937, I was looking forward to trying my luck on trout for the first time. Tales I heard only served to stir my interest, particularly when references were made to steelhead or huge rainbows which showed up each spring.

Most fishermen back then didn't really know how to catch a steelhead legally. (That still holds true with a lot of fishermen of today.) But kids those days found ways to capture them.

The easiest way to learn about trout fishing, I figured, was to tag along with some of the natives and see how it was done. When trout became a spring topic I was raring to go. My newfound friends in school, however, either failed to recognize that there were supposed to be specific seasons or were content to ignore them, along with the legal fishing methods.

Completely ignorant of the fact that opening of trout season was still a month away, I joined a couple of kids who lived out in the Mitchell Creek area. Riding my bicycle that distance, I was filled with anticipation. By the time I met Frank and Bob on the stream, visions of my first trout catch were dancing through my mind.

It didn't dawn on me that anything could be amiss when they headed away from the main stream to one of the smaller tributaries way back in the brush. There we dangled worms in a number of small pools, then trudged noisily from one to another. Considering the vibrations we set off in the ground and water, it is no wonder nobody caught a trout — not even a little one. Trout weren't dumb back then, either, season or no season.

Finally tiring of the inactivity, Frank and Bob confided they had a sure-fire trick, one their father always used whenever he was fish-hungry. Sneaking to the site of an old mill building, they pulled a board loose and a torrent of water was released. "We'll come so back a little later," explained Frank, "because we don't want Mark Craw getting nosey." (I later learned that they were referring to the old game warden who seemed to be everywhere in Grand Traverse County.)

In due time, we sneaked back and replaced the retaining board. Just below the mill were the remains of what had been an old wooden spillway. The boys carefully lifted some of the loose planks and there, left high and dry, were two whopper steelhead trout!

"We better take these home because it wouldn't be a good idea for you to have to carry them on your bike," explained my companions. "We'll bring some of it to school tomorrow cooked. It will be great," said Bob. They did, too, and it was, although at the time I had no idea I was tasting illegal, baked steelhead.

Dad, of course blew his top when I happened to mention what had happened. When he cooled down a bit, he explained that the trout season was still nearly a month away and, besides, that was no way to go fishing for trout.

Thoroughly chagrinned, I avoided further contact with my two earlier friends and got acquainted with a new one the kids all called "Moose," although he wasn't built at all like one.

When trout season was close to opening, he invited me to go along to check a creek that flowed into the Boardman River.

We pussyfooted along and watched closely under half-submerged logs that should shelter trout. It didn't take long before Moose stopped and pointed excitedly at a huge tail fanning slowly in the current.

The steelhead's head was up under a cross-log and it couldn't see us at all. While I was admiring that enormous trophy fish, Moose disappeared. He showed up shortly with a stubby-handled spear that looked somewhat the worse for rust.

I watched in amazement as Moose carefully sneaked up close, then with a quick thrust, impaled the big trout on the deadly spear tines. There was a lot of splashing and a little swearing as Moose hauled the dying trout out onto the creek bank. Moose decided he better take it home for his mother to cook and said he would bring some to school, a story I found to be getting uneasily familiar.

A seeming eternity later, the trout season finally opened. Considering my previous experiences, I decided to go out alone and peddled my trusty bicycle from Traverse City out to Mitchell Creek.

Dad and I had both earlier bought hollow, steel, telescoping rods with reels from Nesbitt's hardware store. I also took Dad's advice and had tied on a gut leader to the end of my line which, he explained, would make it hard for a trout to see. I also had a full can of worms which I had dug from our garden spot on East Ninth Street.

Striving to remember what else Dad had said, I carefully sneaked up on each pool in the creek and just as carefully lowered my worm bait into the quiet current.

My first such attempt brought an electrifying vibration up the line. I waited a second or two then heaved away. Out came a writhing brook trout 8.5 inches long — my very first real trout! I was utterly fascinated and admired its gorgeous coloration for minutes before finally laying it gently in my wicker creel.

Later on, far up the stream, and without another legal-sized trout to show for my efforts, I ran into Moose. He was fishless, so I proudly showed him my special trout, something that somehow failed to impress him. He was obviously a big game fisherman, no matter what he had to do to get a big trout.

Taking turns fishing on down the creek, we came to one quiet pool and Moose spotted a big steelhead fanning gently in the current. "Boy, I wish I had my spear!" he whispered excitedly.

Since he didn't have, though, I decided to see if I could get the trout to hit a worm, an attempt Moose informed me was doomed to failure. "Steelheads won't bite!" he stated firmly.

After floating a worm within inches of the big trout with no response, I was about to agree with Moose. "I'm going to try a spinner," I finally told him. I tied on a little silver one that was in a box in the bottom of my creel.

Moose got downstream and hid in the brush where he could watch my spinner as I lowered it into the current. He finally informed me it was spinning directly in front of the big trout's nose. I held it there for several minutes, then just as I began moving it away, sure that it wouldn't work, an amazing thing happened. The trout grabbed the spinner!

Shocked, I struck back and found myself with a big, mad steelhead on the other end of my line. I held him there for a few seconds as he thrashed around the little pool. Finally, with my steel rod threatening to break, I had to give line and the fish began to head downstream.

As the fish vanished under a log I thought it was all over. Then I heard a big splash, followed by a loud whoop from Moose. There he stood, holding my trophy trout in one hand, line still dangling from its jaw. In the other hand was a sturdy club.

When the steelhead came out near him on a shallow riffle, Moose had instinctively grabbed the club and belted the fish as its head and back protruded from the water. There was really no other way I could have landed it.

Figuring I had caught the steelhead legally, I hung it from my bicycle handlebars and began to peddle homeward, despite dire warnings from Moose that I might run into Mark Craw.

Sure enough, only a short distance along my route, the uniformed officer stepped out of the roadside brush. I slowed down, expecting the worst, but was greeted with a smile and a hearty, "That's a real nice fish you've got there, young man."

At that moment, Mark Craw became a lifelong friend. I wouldn't have broken a fish or game law after that for anything in the world!

Spilling a whole load of ice on Boughey Hill was
not exactly planned by anybody.

HAIL THE ICE MAN!

DESPITE THE FACT that there was absolutely nothing I would rather have done than go fishing or hunting all the time, I decided rather reluctantly that I should get at least a summertime job. That, after all, would also make it easier for me to have the money to pursue some of my main interests.

Finding work in the late 1930s, though, was not an easy task as just about any job available was quickly taken, no matter what it might pay. I was lucky, though.

When Dad first came to Traverse City in late 1936, he had to room for a few weeks with Henry Houdek and his wife over on West Eighth Street. It was right across from the high school where I had just finished up my sophomore year. It also put me in a good position to learn that Henry was looking for an extra iceman to work for him and his son, Amil, in their natural ice delivery business. It was called, aptly enough, the Houdek Ice Company.

In 1937, I didn't have much of a build. I stood about 5-foot-6 and might have weighed as much as 120 pounds with my boots on. I was able to convince Henry, however, that I was a lot stronger than I looked so he decided to at least give me a chance. I would be working as an assistant to Bill Loveland, which turned out to be an experience all its own.

My transportation to and from the job was my shiny bicycle, which I rode to Houdek's where I climbed aboard one of the ice trucks.

Cedar Lake at Greilickville was the source of our ice supply. It was cut there each winter when it had thickened sufficiently and was stored away in a rather lopsided ice house that sat on shore just to the west of the present public fishing access site.

To keep it from melting, liberal amounts of sawdust covered the 200-pound chunks. Each morning we had to dig out a new supply of ice, then wash it off with a hose that took its water supply from the lake depths. Because of their weight, the big ice slabs had to be quartered so we could lift them onto the trucks. Saws and ice picks did the job in relatively neat fashion but swinging those 50-pound chunks was hot, hard work.

All of us usually stripped down to the waist to cool off but it was still hot work, even under the early morning sun. Amil Houdek had a helper, too. He was Harold Carnahan, a muscular young fellow who had won the Silver Gloves division of the regional Golden Gloves boxing competition.

Harold and I often horsed around some when the older fellows weren't paying too much attention but sometimes it went a little far. For example, one day when I wasn't looking, Harold sneaked up behind me and stuck the water hose down inside the rear of my pants. Those chilly waters from Cedar Lake cooled me down immediately!

Trucks we used in 1937 were old even then. They were of Model-T heritage, with gas and spark levers on the steering wheel and it took a certain touch to keep ours running. The idea of letting Bill do all of the driving, though, got to me and I soon talked him into letting me learn to drive,

When I got the hang of it, Bill let me drive all the time. That was an extra adventure far as I was concerned, even though it did result in several unusual happenings during that summer.

One occurred when I approached Front Street from a side street and the brakes failed momentarily. The truck poked out halfway across the street but, luckily, no traffic was coming. I quickly put it into reverse and backed up. How was I to know another vehicle had driven up behind me? I crinkled his hood neatly with the truck bed.

Fortunately, the other driver felt he was at fault for following too closely so we both drove off our separate ways without having to call the police. That was an extra break for me because at that time I didn't even have a driver's license. Whew!

Far more spectacular was the time Bill and I were delivering ice on the south side of Traverse City. I was on my way up Boughey Hill when the old truck stalled. In a show of youthful proficiency, I quickly restarted the engine, the truck gave a tremendous lurch and the entire load of ice neatly crashed through the splintered end gate and fell to the street.

Bill, who was an old fellow of about 50 or 60 then, was noted for his salty language. Right then, I learned a whole string of new expletives, although none were the kind you could ever dare use in mixed company, even now.

There was nothing we could do, though, but get out, saw up all of the ice into even smaller pieces and load it back on the balky truck.

Most of our delivery route was marked out for us by the posting of ice signs in a front window. The housewife who needed 25 or 40 pounds of ice would turn that side of a card out and one of us would go in and fill her icebox.

Side-loading boxes were easiest to fill, although some of the biggest opened from the top, making it necessary to lift a big chunk of ice over before it could be lowered down gently with a pair of ice tongs. The ice itself was carried into a house with a canvas bag somewhat similar to those used in delivering newspapers.

Occasionally, I would have to take part of the food out of an icebox in order to have enough space for the ice, then put things back wherever I could find room.

Ice boxes varied in their degree of cleanliness, too. Some women kept them spotless while others left a lot to be desired. I can still remember one on East Fourteenth Street that always smelled like dead chickens about to be consigned to the garbage pail.

On my first day of working with Bill, I went up to a house and knocked on the door. Bill immediately yelled at me for wasting time. "Just go right in!" he shouted. "They've got a card up so they're looking for you!"

Well, most times that was right. There were other times, however, when barging right into a house proved to be rather embarrassing. As an example, the time I walked right in on a pair of honeymooners. At least they were acting like that.

Another time, lugging my usual chunk of ice, I walked into a kitchen via the back door and ran right into a girl I had gone to school with the last semester. In those days, not all of the houses had bathtubs and this was one of them.

She was standing, stark naked, in a galvanized tub of water, right in the middle of the kitchen, obviously taking a bath. When I wandered in, she calmly reached for a big towel hanging on a nearby chair and just stood there waiting for me to complete my work.

I, of course, blushed furiously and came very close to dropping 40 pounds of ice on my toes. I swear, the heat from my face must have melted a couple pounds off the block of ice before I filled her box and fled back to the truck!

Some of our customers were confirmed grouches, according to what Bill said. For some reason, he used to let me take care of those, maybe figuring be would just get into more trouble if he made the deliveries. This backfired on him the first day he sent me into a house occupied by an old widow woman.

When I had finished loading the icebox, she asked if I could spare a minute to eat a piece of fresh huckleberry pie with a scoop of whipped cream on it. Could I ever! Bill about had fits when I came out wiping the berry juice off my mouth. "All she ever did was scream at me'" he lamented.

Part of the benefit of carrying ice was in the pleasure it always brought neighborhood youngsters. Invariably, when we stopped and began to saw and pick the ice into delivery sizes, kids would come swarming around.

"Hey, Mr. Iceman, can we have some ice?" they would shout. The fact that they recognized me as an iceman made a real impression on my youthful mind and I always obliged by chipping off a little extra. They generally went away sucking happily on the ice.

Even after all these years, I also enjoy chewing on ice cubes after finishing up a cool drink. Guess it brings back a bit of nostalgia that way, too.

Maybe it was the snacks that came my way at the variety of houses where I delivered ice or perhaps it was the steady exercise but by summer's end I had filled out considerably and taken on more muscle. I was also deeply tanned from the episodes at the Cedar Lake ice-house. I was even a little richer, although not much by today's standards.

Working three days a week, I started out at $6 a week. Finally, getting up my nerve about midsummer, I asked for a raise. Henry Houdek pondered it over long and carefully, then raised my pay to $8 a week. In 1937, for a kid with a summer job, that was really living!

Too bad electric refrigerators had to louse things up not long afterwards. With their arrival came the demise of the old-time iceman.

There were other changes around Cedar Lake, too, some of which offered fabulous opportunities if you had the foresight to look into the future. One came a year or two later when Dad came home from work shaking his head.

"One of the guys at work has some 100-foot lots he wants to sell on Cedar Lake," he said, explaining they adjoined the old Houdek Ice Company icehouse. "Only thing, he wants $50 apiece for them. What would anybody ever do with land like that? I told him I wasn't interested."

Howard Blonshine did his trout fishing from a
window of the old Keystone Dam.

HOWARD BLONSHINE

FISHING OUT OF a window overlooking a top-notch trout stream isn't exactly the normal way this sport is enjoyed.

Howard Blonshine saw nothing wrong with it, though, and freely admitted that while his bosses might frown on the practice, he couldn't see what harm it did. Besides, he caught a lot of brown trout that way to help feed his family.

Back in the late 1930s, Fred Swaney and I were still struggling to get through high school in Traverse City, a task we finally managed to accomplish. Summers though, were heavenly, without such distractions except when we had jobs. Even then, we managed to find enough free time to get in a lot of fishing.

Daytimes we worked at whatever odd jobs we could find to help out with school expenses to come but nights were entirely free. We often took advantage of that to peddle our bicycles from Traverse City south to Keystone Dam, the fourth upstream structure to block part of the Boardman River. It was there that Howard Blonshine was the night dam supervisor or whatever his title might have been back then.

Fred was some sort of shirt-tail relative of Howard's and that is how I got acquainted with him, too. Nights at a powerhouse tend to be a little lonesome, particularly in the wee hours of the morning. Since Fred and I often fished until dawn, it gave us plenty of time to visit with Howard.

Howard's technique for trout fishing was simple. He would just use a hand-line with a short leader on the bottom and would bait the hook with a worm most of the time. A bell sinker would hold the lure down on bottom in the current until a brown would swim by, find it and inhale the bait.

By checking the set line once in a while, Howard could tell when there was action down below. He would then, rather unceremoniously, haul the fish up out of the water and in through the powerhouse window. Some of the trout, of course, would fall off first but he wasn't bothered in the least as he knew that, sooner or later, he would probably catch the same trout again, even if it took until the next night, week or month.

When I asked one time how many brown trout he had caught that way, he estimated, rather conservatively, that it was probably a truckload or so over the years. I can easily believe that, considering just the ones I saw him land. Most of the trout were just good frying pan size but quite often he would come up with one good enough for a Che-Ge-Gon plaque, meaning 20 inches or longer. Howard never bothered applying for such at the Traverse City Chamber of Commerce, though, because he caught so many of them.

With Fred and me, though, we literally panted to achieve such an honor as to land a plaque-winning brown trout. We dutifully copied Howard's methods but since he really couldn't see his way clear to let us fish out of the powerhouse windows we had to confine our efforts to the areas outdoors.

Howard used worms for bait most of the time but there was one time of year when he would switch. That was during the so-called "caddis hatch" or when the giant mayflies were in the midst of their mating frenzy. Local barber Art Winnie was responsible for calling them "caddis flies" because it helped him sell the feathered objects he created on hooks at his workbench in the shop.

Fred and I, though, were content to just imitate Howard's method of catching a jar full of the big, cellophane-winged flies with their long, soft bodies. We would then string two or three on a hook and fish them in the turbulent water below the powerhouse. That made good sense because the flies hatching from the muck of Keystone Pond above, would often be swept on through the dam's turbines and provide a bonanza of food-to the trout lying in wait in the waters below.

When a trout would suck in that luscious-looking bait of clustered mayflies on a hook, Fred or I would soon know it by the rhythmic vibrations on a rod. We didn't attempt Howard's method of just hauling the fish up onto the concrete apron on each side of the powerhouse, though, considering that much too risky. Instead, we would gradually work the rod over to the side, then going down below to river level, finally lead the struggling fish into a landing net. We caught a lot of brown trout that way nearly every night we visited Keystone Dam, although most were just pan-sized fish.

Occasionally, though, a bigger brown would show up and surprise us. One night, in fact, I had carelessly laid my rod too close to the edge of the concrete and gone back inside the powerhouse to chat with Howard and Fred. When I looked out again, rod, reel and all had vanished.

In a panic, I got a flashlight and was somewhat relieved to see the entire outfit lying hooked just barely by the reel to a tiny, underwater ledge below. Inches more and it would have been out of sight.

There being no other way to retrieve it, Howard brought out one of his throw lines and by careful maneuvering, managed to hook onto my rod with that outfit. Gingerly then, he was able to raise my rod and reel from the water to where I eagerly grabbed it.

I would have been happy to just find I had my fishing tackle back but was downright delighted to discover I still had the trout on which had pulled it into the water. Fred and I combined forces then to work the fish over to one side and finally scooped it out in a landing net. It proved to be a husky 19-inch brown, just one inch short of qualifying for one of the highly-coveted Che-Ge-Gon plaques. Needless to say, I was still pretty darned happy.

Being of an explorer nature, however, I often went up above to where there was a little secondary side spillway. It was used to take pressure off the main dam in case there was a sudden influx of water brought on by an extra-heavy rainfall. Down below was a shallow little pond into which the spillway dumped its overflow.

By fishing in that current I was often able to snake out an extra brown trout or two, especially when the caddis hatch was in full swing. I never did expect to catch anything too impressive there, which just goes to show that in trout fishing you never really know.

One night after the big hatch had been going for a couple weeks, Fred and I were again trying our luck at Keystone but not having too much activity. The brown trout were apparently full of the big flies and not really interested in swallowing more. Well into early morning, I finally quit fishing near the powerhouse and went to see if anything might be happening below the little side spillway.

It was dark down below and I had forgotten my flashlight but I was sure that wouldn't be necessary, anyhow. I had already strung three of the big mayflies on my hook and had a single split shot up above to make sure it would sink to bottom when I lowered it into the light current.

There was only a short pause before I felt a light tapping out there in the darkness and I confidently lifted the rod, expecting to flip a little brown trout out onto the hank. It was a real shock to find a weight that was unbelievably heavy on the other end of my line. This was no little one at all!

That was the beginning of a real power struggle out there in the darkness. An occasional explosion on the surface let me know I had a real mad trout hooked and there was no way of knowing how big it might be.

How long the struggle went on I have no idea because it was far too dark for me to see my watch. Maybe it was 15 minutes or maybe longer, I don't really know. Eventually, though, I was able to work the trout in close enough to take a poke at it with my landing net. It promptly fell out and I very nearly panicked, even though the fish was still hooked. That happened twice before I was finally calm enough to slide the big fish into the mesh and lifted it out of the water.

Even so, I still had to struggle back up the bank to the dam lights to see what was in the net. It was, I saw then, one whopper of a brown trout. When finally measuring it, the fish stretched out to 24.5 inches long, a real trophy!

I half-ran back to the main powerhouse where Fred was sitting inside reading a magazine. I pounded on the window and can still see him turning around slowly, then his mouth falling open in disbelief as he saw that big brown trout still flopping in my hand. My watch said it was 2:30 a.m.

Howard's casual response of "Nice fish," should be about what I might have expected, considering the number of trout he had hauled in over the years.

"Nice?" I shrieked. "It's fabulous!" Fred agreed wholeheartedly with me, even though I thought I saw him turning a slight shade of green as in envy.

Leo Thiel thought so, too, when I proudly pedaled my bicycle down to Trude's Hardware store at the corner of Front and Union streets the next morning as soon as they opened up. He measured my trout carefully and confirmed that it was really 24.5 inches long, then made out a form which qualified me for my first-ever award of a Che-Ge-Gon plaque. I was proud enough to bust the buttons off my best fishing shirt!

I was doubly happy to let Trude's put the fish on display in a pan of ice out in front of the store so passersby could also enjoy proof of my prowess with fishing tackle.

It was something of an anti-climax when Leo phoned me at the end of the summer to come down to the store to get my first-place prize for the biggest brown trout caught that season. It was a fine Shakespeare casting reel that I still have and use occasionally.

Even at that, I still made out better than Keystone Dam itself. Sometime in the early 1960s, a record rainfall proved to be too much for the Boardman River. It not only overflowed its banks but, in the process, washed out the little side spillway dam where I had landed my biggest brown trout.

Howard Blonshine had retired in 1949 before that happened, though. Probably a good thing, too, because the Traverse City fathers decided to not rebuild Keystone Dam. Instead, they removed all signs of the historic old structure and today it is difficult to even find where it once stood.

Dreams of fishing Platte River finally won out over
a summer job at the old Traverse Hotel.

PLATTE RIVER KEPT CALLING

I N THE LATE 1930s, Fred Swaney and I took our trout
fishing very seriously, particularly once summer had
released us from school. Every possible moment we
could manage, we were out worming some local trout stream
and doing quite well at it.

Even with the vexing problem of summer jobs, we still were
able to somehow work around them so as to not miss very
many opportunities outdoors.

One summer both of us were toiling away as bellhops at the
old Traverse Hotel which then sat at the corner of Front and
Union streets in Traverse City. I also had the privilege of
running the elevator up and down the five floors and enjoyed
that as I could then create my own kind of "fun."

The elevator in that old hotel would give fits to today's
OSHA and other governmental safety groups. it was controlled by a heavy hemp rope which would be lifted or lowered
in order to get the elevator going or stopped.

I found when it was time to head down from the fifth floor,
where the Farmer's Mutual Insurance Company office was
located, that I could give a mighty heave on the rope and the
elevator would drop like a rock. It generally left my passengers
gasping for breath but I always managed to reverse the rope

and stop the plunge before we hit bottom in the basement.

That kind of excitement, though, was nothing compared to the mysteries of trout fishing, especially when Fred and I decided to explore Platte River over in Benzie County. On short excursions, we merely went armed with rods and creels and hitch-hiked the 25 miles to and from there. That, however, was just sort of a teaser and we got to wondering what might be done if we could spend a solid week fishing that great stream.

Such thoughts finally got the best of us and toward the end of the summer we actually quit our jobs at the hotel, giving owner Lloyd Neuffer some sort of excuse why we both had to leave at the same time. The same explanation must have sounded okay to our parents, too, because Ivan Swaney, Fred's dad, agreed to take us to the Platte with his car and transport our necessary camping gear. (My dad didn't even own a car then, due mostly to having to stretch family finances back then.)

Clark's Mill, located on the upper Platte, north of US-31 and just off Highway 669, to the west, was our favorite water as we could fish either upstream or down and know we were in some great trout water. We set up our little pup tent on the edge of a wooded spot and were fishing within minutes after Mr. Swaney's car vanished enroute back to Traverse City.

Fancying ourselves real sportsmen, we had tied up some beautiful flies (well they looked that way to us) which were mostly nymphs. Although I'm sure they looked like nothing else in the stream, when tossed toward likely-looking spots with our $1.50 Montgomery Ward split bamboo flyrods, some of them even worked. If the flies didn't produce as we waded downstream, we always kept a supply of worms handy. They always worked.

Anyhow, we caught trout — a lot of them. Ones we kept were popped into our creels and eventually ended up at our campsite in the frying pan, the only way we knew how to cook them.

I had borrowed Mom's best cast-iron frying pan for this trip, after promising to take the very best care of it. When it came to clean-up chores, though, getting fried fish leavings loose was something neither of us really enjoyed. That's when I recalled reading something that led me to experiment.

After finishing with the frying, I put the pan back on the campfire and heated it until it was sizzling hot. The article I read had those instructions, then the pan was to be quickly dunked into cold water. The rapid change in temperature was supposed to loosen anything foreign in the pan, leaving it sparkling clean. It all seemed very logical as I took the hot frying pan from the fire and dropped it into a shallow place in the river.

Hey, have you ever watched a cast-iron pan explode? Ours did exactly that, leaving me trying to dream up some explanation later on for my mother. Heck, why didn't the writer of the article I had read explain you weren't supposed to try that with a cast-iron pan?

Actually, Fred and I fared quite well in the food department, considering that we mostly ate fried trout and rounded out that diet with pancakes made in the same frying pan. Fortunately, we did have another aluminum pan that belonged to Fred's mother, so we were not left completely helpless by the demise of the one I had brought along. Taking no further chances, we cleaned that one with sand from the river bottom each day.

We also had a pretty good deal when we discovered a milkman was delivering to a nearby house. We flagged him down and had him leave a quart of milk every day just outside of our tent, then kept it cold in the river. Our records showed we caught something over 70 trout during our week of camping and we must have eaten nearly all of them. Otherwise, how could you explain that our complete grocery bill amounted to only $1.50 apiece for the whole week?

Clark's Mill, of course is long gone from the upper Platte River now, although there is still some sign of where it was located. A very fast run comes rushing through a rocky, narrow spot that still contains a deep hole. But, in no way can it compare to what used to be there when it came to holding big trout.

It did rain occasionally while Fred and I camped there. One day I can still recall vividly, I hurried out of the tent to reach a spot on the board catwalk extended across the river, right below the mill. It was perfect for floating a worm into the back currents which swirled along both sides. Even without weight, the bait easily drifted to bottom where I knew trout were waiting.

A night of rain always puts trout on a feeding spree, particularly for worms which are washed into a stream. The Platte was no different in this regard so I wasn't surprised when I quickly snaked out an 11-inch brook trout, one of the best we caught that week. On my next cast, something bigger grabbed the whole nightcrawler I had hooked in the middle.

The trout quickly jumped, spraying water and shaking his head. I could see the vivid red stripe down his sides, although rather late for that color this long after the spawning season.

Moving quickly off the catwalk to the bank, I worked into a better position where the trout was upstream of me and fighting the current as well as the bend of my rod. The rainbow finally tired enough for me to slide him into the landing net. It was a 19-incher, best of the whole week!

Fred had picked this morning to sleep a little longer but woke up quickly when I waved that big trout in his face as he climbed out of the tent. I enjoyed that, too!

When not in operation, however, the mill yielded some fine trout at times. The current had dug out a huge hole that extended back upstream under the mill building itself. I would frequently climb up on the mill structure itself when nobody was around. There, at least ten feet above the water, I would aim a dangling nightcrawler into a little foot-square hole below. It would drift down into the dark recesses and be sucked farther out of sight. The bait was always inhaled by something big and lively.

Although I knew I was always in an impossible spot to ever land a big trout from there, I always enjoyed trying. Actually, I was just hoping to see what had been hooked but it never happened. That whopper of a trout was probably a reluctant rainbow that decided to linger on after other spawners had returned to Lake Michigan, miles downstream.

In the 1930s, the Platte was also a pretty good brook trout stream and sometimes yielded one as large as 18 inches. As I continued to fish the river, though, an occasional brown trout would show up in the creel.

One day during that same period, I was fishing the stream alone and finished up my 15-trout daily limit just before arriving downstream at the old log building which was then serving as headquarters of the Platte River Rearing Station. It was also home to Harman Galvin who headed up the operation for what was then the Department of Conservation.

Harman and I had become friends not long before so I wanted to stop in to see him and, of course, show off my catch of trout. Among my fish were a couple of late rainbows in the 19-inch size and I was pretty proud to have caught them. I was quite surprised, however, when he dug down through my catch and hauled out a couple of foot-lonq brown trout. "Where did you get these?" he asked. When I told him I had caught them from Platte River, too, he said they were the first brown trout he had ever seen in the stream.

From that time on, as brown trout became more plentiful in the Platte, brookies went into a decline. For a time, so did the steelhead population, although part of that was the steady predation of natives in the area to spear the big, silvery trout out as often as possible each spring.

Platte River itself has undergone plenty of other changes during the past half-century and not all have been for the better. The huge new Platte River Anadramous Fish Hatchery now blocks the river a half-mile below where Clark's Mill once sat. Run by the Department of Natural Resources, it is largely devoted to raising coho salmon to release size.

While the coho and chinook salmon have revitalized fishing on Lake Michigan and the other Great Lakes, these introductions from the Pacific ocean have caused any number of problems for the DNR as well as property owners who have built homes and cottages along the river. Erosion and enrichment of the water have filled in the deepest holes and constant chemical treatments of the stream to kill sea lamprey larvae have largely wiped out the once-heavy mayfly hatches.

Change in everything is inevitable, but until we have lost something entirely we really don't begin to appreciate what we once had.

Still, Platte River — the way it used to be — is continuing to provide many fine memories for a couple of now-grown-up kids, as well as many others.

THE GAME WARDENS

CONSIDERING THE HARD economic times in the 1930s, it should have been no surprise when I found some of my school acquaintances and a lot of their parents were confirmed poachers.

Dad, however, convinced me early on that outdoor laws were made for a reason and the game wardens charged with enforcing them were really our friends. That explanation was further strengthened when I frequently bumped into two of them while either fishing or hunting.

Mark Craw seemed to be all over Grand Traverse County, no matter where I went. The same held true in Benzie County where Rex Joslin was the game warden. It didn't take me very long to get acquainted with both men and to decide they were firm but fair. Neither would tolerate deliberate law violations but when an honest mistake was made, there were some exceptions.

Beginning as he did, in 1900, Mark was one of Michigan's first official game wardens so he already had learned most of the tricks of the trade before I ever met him. As a teenager, though, I was quite fascinated with the man as well as his most unusual "partner."

He owned a huge dog which contained wolf blood. Mark called him "Valentine," because that's the day the dog was born in Manistee. Mark eventually acquired the animal when he was a year old and already weighed 135 pounds. The dog had never been in a house and was as close to his wolf-dog background as would be allowed. Gentleness and kindly behavior by Mark, though, won Valentine's affection and devotion.

Despite an awesome appearance, Valentine was a perfect gentleman and could not, in any way, be called a vicious dog. He became Mark's constant companion and proved highly valuable. Wherever they went, man and dog won respect and admiration, for they came close to being an unbeatable combination.

Through Valentine's eyes, Mark became able to "see" in the dark. Deer shiners and illegal trout spearers no longer found advantage in night activities. Trappers who thought illegal pelts were well hidden behind special wall areas got an unpleasant surprise. Valentine's nose could pick out such places with unerring accuracy.

Overall, the dog's well-developed dog-wolf senses gave Mark a tremendous advantage and many a potential violator wisely decided to remain within the law. It just didn't pay to poach in Mark Craw's territory!

The man and dog had many friends in northern Michigan. Anytime they came to Traverse City they followed a very special route down Front Street. Valentine had a number of stops in the two blocks between Park and Union streets, during which he successfully mooched candy, meat scraps and other tidbits from admirers. Sleder's meat market could always be depended upon to provide an oxtail or something else equally tasty for Valentine. The last stop, however, was always at the drugstore (then at the corner of Front and Union) for dessert. It was a chocolate ice cream cone which, not surprisingly, lasted for only one giant gulp.

Mark, himself, was noted for his strict enforcement of even

the smallest violation of the game and fish laws. One time he arrested Tom Cromley for keeping a bluegill a quarter of an inch too short when those fish had to be at least six inches long.

"He didn't tolerate any kind of law violation," Tom told me later. "But I got even with him. I married his daughter, Jane!" He and Mark often chuckled over that later on.

One day, while casting a spoon for pike at the Boardman Lake tressle, I hooked a huge smallmouth bass, the biggest I had ever seen. Sure that it was well over five pounds, I looked at the fish longingly, wishing I could keep it, even though bass season didn't open for a week .

As I reluctantly slid the fish back into the water and it swam back to freedom, there came a voice from the brush behind me. "That was sure a dandy bass, kid!" It was, of course, Mark Craw who had seen the whole thing. I was startled but happy I had decided to stay within the law.

Fred Swaney and I had a sort of springtime ritual which we followed while in high school. On the Saturday before the trout season was to open, the two of us would hitchhike to Platte River in order to check out the run of steelhead in that clear little stream.

We always carried our shotguns along in order to try shooting a few crows, too, but had no problems with rides back then. Today, you would stand by the road for a long time with a gun before anybody would give you a lift.

No matter when we went, though, it seemed that we always encountered Rex Joslin. He dutifully checked our hunting licenses and always reminded us that steelhead shooting would not be a good idea.

The stretch of stream from the state trout rearing station on up to Clark's Mill was always full of huge steelhead. Fred and I literally panted at the prospect of having to wait another whole week before we could start fishing for the big spawners which had just run up out of Lake Michigan.

Opening day always found us camped on the deepest hole on that part of the Platte and we began to fish at midnight. We didn't catch much in the dark but knew that wading fishermen, both upstream and down would startle enough of the big fish into the pool we had staked out. Later on, after they had calmed down, the trout could be enticed to strike a Colorado spinner worked right in front of their noses. The majority of fishermen back then had no idea steelhead could be caught by legitimate fishing methods.

Snagging was a way of life for most but some thought even that was too slow and resorted to using big gaffs which were then legal to use. That became very apparent when Fred hooked a big steelie and it headed off downstream with him in hot pursuit. Before he could catch up, though, a man stepped out of the brush and into the crystal water and swung his gaff.

As he lifted the thrashing trout out of the river, we could hear him yell to a companion, "Hey, this one's got a spinner and a line in its mouth!" He appeared to be shocked to find Fred thrashing toward him and reeling in line. "I'll be damned!" was the guy's final comment as Fred retrieved his 8-pounder and headed back toward our hot fishing hole.

When fishing a spot with quite a few big fish in it, however, you may occasionally foul-hook a trout without meaning to do so. That happened to me on the same day although I didn't realize it right away.

As my steelhead finally left the hole and began to swim on downstream, Rex Joslin appeared out of somewhere. He grabbed my landing net and charged into the stream, soon catching up with the trout. A quick swipe of the net and the steelhead was lifted safely from the water.

When Rex brought it back he me, he and I both saw the Colorado spinner had hooked the steelhead alongside the head. From that, he knew I hadn't tried to snag the fish deliberately so he just congratulated me and went on about his business of stalking real poachers. That trout, by the way, was only a 3-pounder, the smallest of nine steelhead we caught that way. The others ran up to a whopping 11-pounder!

Gaff-swingers on the Platte that same day, however, removed spawning steelhead by the gunny sack full. That outrage gained so much attention that Lansing lawmakers banned the use of gaffs on every trout stream in Michigan. Rex Joslin's testimony on the matter was one of the main selling points for the law which still remains on the books.

Eventually, Rex retired from his job as a game warden, although by then the title had been changed to "conservation officer." In retirement, he took advantage of many of the outdoor adventures everybody else was enjoying. One such very nearly got him into a lot of trouble.

When I ran across him one day, he confided that he could finally see where a sportsman could make an honest mistake. His problem took place on Little Platte Lake where he had a spread of decoys out for flight ducks. As a big flock of bluebills set their wings, preparatory to landing among the blocks, Rex stood up and shot twice.

"I couldn't believe it when I found there were seven ducks laying dead on the water!" he said. With the daily limit only five, he found himself anxiously looking over his shoulder to see if there might be a game warden watching. "For the very first time, I knew exactly how a violator must feel!" he said.

Rex said he immediately hid two of the ducks in the grass, then sat there for a while wondering what he could possibly do. Not wanting to see the extras go to waste, though, he finally hiked back out and took his five ducks home. He then went to the post office and bought his wife a duck stamp, picked up a hunting license for her, too, then went back for the two problem ducks he had left at the lake. "That's all I could think of to do," he said. "I hope it was right."

Mark Craw also took part in a duck mishap before he

retired. Frances Olson let me in on that little secret which had been related by her father, Oren Olson, who had a resort on Spider Lake.

Oren and Mark liked to hunt for ducks on Round Lake (now called Skegemog) and were enjoying a great day in the shooting blind they had built there. With the daily limit then ten ducks, Oren figured they must be getting close to that figure.

"I finally asked Mark how many we had to go and he said one more would do it," Oren related. "When a big greenhead drake came in, I shot it and we were finished for the day."

On heading back to their respective homes, however, Mark said he only wanted two of the ducks for himself and his wife. Oren therefore took the remaining mallards and went about plucking them. He was understandably shocked to find, though, that there were 19 ducks in the day's bag.

"Imagine that," he commented later. "And there I was in the same blind with a game warden!"

A 20-pound canvas kayak made it possible to run
a trapline on the Boardman River.

KAYAK PAID FOR ITSELF

S AN AVID teenage reader who eagerly devoured the northern novels of James Hendryx and Harold Titus, I also found a number of outdoor magazines fascinating.

One of my favorites in the 1930s was Field & Stream but I had to give it long and careful thought whether to continue when that publication raised its news stand rate from ten cents all the way up to 15 cents! How could anybody possibly think of such a price, even for those great outdoor stories?

In the end, though, I managed to scrounge up the extra nickel. To make up for it, though, I read every word in the magazine, including all of the classified ads. That, as it turned out, was how I found a real enticement.

One ad was for a kit to build a lightweight kayak said to weigh only 20 pounds. The only drawback was its cost, a whopping $20 or $1 a pound. Unthinkable!

Considering its many uses, however, I finally justified its purchase and sent off for it. It would, I told myself, be ideal for all kinds of fishing, duck hunting in places I was unable to reach otherwise and, uppermost in my mind, it would allow me to run a trapline. The latter, if successful as I was sure it would be, would enrich me when I sold the many valuable furs

I would be able to take.

Not being sure Mom and Dad would understand it all, I didn't mention it to them. Mom was thus quite amazed when a delivery truck pulled up in front of our house one day and the driver assured her the long, mysterious package was already paid for.

She hauled it down to our basement through the two big doors behind the house, then questioned me thoroughly when I got home from school. Even then, she and Dad weren't really convinced I had made a good investment.

But I eagerly tackled the task of assembling my new water-craft. It consisted of some rather frail-looking stringers 12-feet long, plus equally fragile-type ribs. After assembling them according to the instructions, I tacked on a canvas covering and installed the long cockpit.

It actually came out looking like a real boat! Once I had applied waterproofing, which shrunk the canvas and tight-ened it into place, then applied a coat of brown paint for camouflage, my new craft was ready. I was finally a boat owner!

Living on East Ninth Street, three blocks from Boardman Lake and even farther from the river, was no real problem, even if our family did lack a car. Getting to and from the water was as simple as shouldering the 20-pound kayak and taking off on foot.

For my boat's maiden voyage, I put in above the Union Street Dam. Admittedly, it did feel rather strange, sitting in the bottom of the kayak but that gave it more stability, making it very difficult to ever tip it over. I found, too, that I could travel quite rapidly with the aid of the double-bladed paddle.

The paddle came apart, too, and made into two single paddles. When Fred Swaney discovered my new craft we found the two of us could fairly sizzle along with both of us paddling. The fact that there were no flotation chambers in the kayak never even occurred to us as we went exploring with it in all kinds of hazardous places.

One day, for example, we decided to check out the deadstream side of the Boardman River which sort of lazied on into the lake to the east of the main channel. It was full of stumps, submerged logs and a host of other hidden, underwater snags.

We threaded our way between those obstacles as best we could but one time found ourselves hung up on one persistent snag. Try as we might, we couldn't get quite free. It was with a justified concern that we watched as the canvas in the kayak bottom bulged when we rocked gently to and fro trying to get free of the menace.

It was only when the snag bulge had run the entire length of the craft, passing under both of us, that we finally managed to slide off safely, without punching a hole through the fabric. That, we both agreed, was a hair-raising adventure we didn't care to repeat.

Having tested the steadyness and strength of my kayak, we set out on new dangers, although we didn't think of them that way. Often, we would paddle right down the middle of Boardman Lake, seeking to find some kind of fish to catch. Came opening of the duck season, we had no hesitation, either, in loading the kayak down with our own bodies wearing heavy shell vests. Shotguns, duck decoys and other gear designed to help us fool ducks, coots or whatever else we might encounter, were also stowed aboard. Nobody thought about life vests then.

Somebody up above was certainly watching over a pair of foolish youngsters who thought nothing of tempting fate that way. Anyhow, we never did swamp the little boat or even punch a hole in its fragile canvas covering during our times on the water.

Trapping, however, was my main reason for building the

kayak in the first place. I knew there were a lot of muskrats in Boardman Lake and the river system and I intended to catch my share of them.

Since there were quite a few other trappers working the lake and upper river, however, I looked around and discovered nobody was trapping the river inside Traverse City itself. That, I decided, would become my own personal trapping grounds.

Accordingly, after I had invested what little was left of my "riches" in a dozen leghold traps at 50 cents apiece, I laid out my trapline. It began in the quiet waters above the Union Street Dam and extended all the way up to Boardman Lake where the train tressle crossed over the river flowing out.

That part of the impounded Boardman River contained a number of deadheads which poked up from bottom and left just enough above water for muskrats to use as feeding platforms. The best ones had small mounds of water weeds piled on them as evidence the little furbearers frequently visited them.

On those I placed a trap where I was sure a muskrat would step into it, then jump off into the water and quickly drown. There was no use in trying to catch the animals where they would remain alive and maybe twist off a leg and escape. That, I figured, would not benefit either the muskrat or me.

I also soon discovered it wasn't a good idea to set a trap on any such snag near shore where it might be reached by one of the kids who were poking along there each day. How could they know that one of my visible traps wasn't meant to be pulled loose and taken home as an easy souvenir? After losing a couple traps that way, I began to set in places that could be reached only by boat and my trap loss ceased.

To entice a muskrat to visit my trap sets, I often baited them with a half-apple on a stick which I poked into one of the snag cracks to keep it from floating away. That worked fine and resulted in steady catches of fur for me.

Most of my muskrats were of normal size and brought me between 75 cents and a dollar each when I had stretched them dry and shipped them off to Sears & Roebuck in an old gunny sack. The company paid promptly and I was happy to get their checks, figuring I was making good money for the work involved.

The first fall of trapping, though, produced two huge muskrats. Nearly twice the size of an ordinary, adult animal, they blundered into my traps set just above the Union Street Dam. I had to fashion special stretchers in order to dry their fur and was delighted when each one brought me an amazing $3.75 from my mail sales.

At the other end of the scale, however, there were often pelts of lesser quality and size, some paying me as little as 50 cents apiece. The lowest price I ever got, though, was a muskrat pelt that had been badly damaged before I even skinned the animal.

That one had obviously been attacked by a mink which had probably found the muskrat just as it stepped into my trap. The mink had bitten and slashed the muskrat to such an extent that it looked like the unfortunate animal had been cut repeatedly with a razor. I still decided to stretch and dry the pelt to see what it might be worth to a fur dealer. That one only got me ten cents and I figured I was lucky to get even that much.

The mink, of course, aroused my curiosity and I did my best to find some way to catch it, too. But my best efforts there failed and I never did manage to come close to getting that one. It did serve to stir my interest and I later went exploring on some of the local creeks where I knew mink also lived.

On one upper branch of the Asylum Creek, I found a runway coming out of the water and decided it must have been made by a mink. A trap placed just beneath the water's surface there did the job and one evening when I checked the trap I found a fine mink drowned in that set.

That thrilled me no end because his pelt brought me the unbelievable price of $30! Unfortunately, the one mink was all I was able to catch that first year, although I certainly tried to catch others. Mink obviously, were a lot more wary than muskrats, as well as being more scarce.

Trapping has always been a lot of hard work but it has served to give many a youngster some extra spending money. In the 1930s it also helped many adults to just survive from effects of the Great Depression.

I always checked my traps morning and night on the weekends but during school had to settle for evenings only. To carry my kayak back and forth before school just wasn't practical each day. I did religiously check my trapline at least once a day in all kinds of weather and made sure I used only drowning sets. I didn't want any of the furbearers to suffer unduly.

Picking up my fur catch was only the easy part. The animals had to be dried thoroughly afterwards, then carefully skinned and every bit of fat removed from the pelts. They were then turned inside out and put on stretching boards of the right size.

At first I used wooden stretchers which I had laborously carved to the perfect shape and size, then had a better idea. I collected some corrugated cardboard boxes from local stores and brought them home. There, using a razor blade, I cut out stretchers to whatever size I needed.

Since the fur was dry by then I could easily pull the pelts over the stretcher of a perfect size and hold them there with long pins or slender nails. That made it unnecessary to nail them solidly into wood. They were easily removed when it was time to ship the pelts off for sale and because I had so many stretchers, I could leave the fur on them as long as wanted.

In addition to being another outlet for my youthful energy,

trapping had other benefits. In running a trapline on a regular basis, it is impossible to not learn a lot about the outdoors and the workings of nature. I became very familiar with not only the habits of the muskrats but with many other wildlife species I was able to observe. That included the importance of the right kind of habitat which was then so abundant in the Grand Traverse region.

Even today, a few youngsters still manage to gain a part of their education on a trapline. Opportunities may be shrinking, however, and some misinformed people oppose the use of fur garments, even though it has always been a renewable resource. Fur, in fact, helped to pioneer this nation of ours.

A wild ride from Ford Island was finally
accomplished through the skills of Fred Birdsey.

FRED BIRDSEY WAS TALENTED

A S A KID, one of the first people I met in Traverse City was Fred Birdsey. He had a barbershop on South Union Street in what is still referred to as "Old Town."

Fred's shop was just around the corner from where we lived on East Ninth Street. Mom sent me over there as often as necessary for one of his 25-cent haircuts, which was a pretty good deal even in the early 1930s.

It was a ritual I didn't really object to, because the little barbershop walls held a wonderful collection of used shotguns and rifles which he also sold. While waiting for my turn in the chair, I longingly looked them over, hoping someday to collect enough money to buy one of them. (I eventually did.)

Barbering must have really agreed with Fred because he began in 1918 and the last time I checked on him in 1994, he was still at it! He gave up the Traverse City location, next to where Zobel's Dairy was then in production, and eventually moved out to 80 acres he bought near Grawn. A house and little barbershop there were built next to a nice pond he dug in between. He did slow down slightly, though, as he got older and cut hair just two afternoons a week.

Since he didn't cut hair on Sundays, Fred sometimes invited me to share in one of his numerous outdoor adventures.

Included was the time we took Fred Swaney along on what turned out to be a wild boat ride back from Ford Island after a duck hunt. (The island, in West Grand Traverse Bay, was later referred to as "Marion Island," then more recently as "Power Island.")

Back in the 1930s, the island was still heavily wooded and bald eagles nested there. They probably thrived on not only the abundant fish in the bay but rounded out their diets with some of the many ducks living around the island's shores. It was those waterfowl which prompted us to take a run out there from Bowers Harbor and set out a few decoys off the west shore of the scenic little island.

The ducks, however, pretty much refused to be fooled by our wooden decoys. After I shot the only one, which turned out to be a merganser not fit to eat, we decided we better head back home. Although we two kids didn't recognize the danger of a storm fast approaching, Fred Birdsey did.

"If that motor hadn't started on the first pull, we would have been in real trouble!" he said later. "I never realized what big boulders there are on that side of the island and we were lucky to make it back to the Peninsula!"

Ignorant of it all, though, Fred Swaney and I just huddled under a tarp in the boat to keep semi-dry as the wind-whipped spray frequently washed over the craft. Fred Birdsey's skill, though, eventually got us safely onto the mainland and he vowed to never again try anything like that with such a small boat.

Raccoons were relatively scarce back in those days but since he could get away from barbering at night, when coon hunting tends to be best, Fred invited me along sometimes to go on a ringtail chase behind one of his big hounds. I don't recall us ever bagging one but we had a lot of fun trying and lost plenty of sleep.

The same pretty well held true when we went fox hunting.

That had to be done in daylight and on Sundays when the barbershop was closed. Winter pelts would be prime so that was the best season, although there was often deep snow to contend with.

No problem with snow drifts, either. Fred was a master trader for guns and just about everything else outdoor-related so he always had at least a few sets of snowshoes around. I had never been on those things before but Fred assured me that it was easy as I strapped on a set of the big webs.

He turned out to be right, too. The first time out I walked approximately nine miles on them and was proud of myself for not falling down too often, even though we didn't shoot any foxes that day.

Somewhere along the line, Fred acquired a fine big hound he called "Bucky." The dog didn't run coons or foxes but was the best big dog I've ever hunted with for snowshoe hares. Fred and I frequently went as far south as the Weidenhammer Swamp and found plenty of the big white bunnies there. The way the hound ran them, however, you had to be plenty fast with a shotgun when the rabbit showed up just ahead of the howling Bucky.

By that time, I also had my own dog, the little beagle "Buster," who was obviously no match for running with a big hound like Bucky. Accordingly, I usually hunted on my own. On one of those jaunts, though, Buster showed a complete lack of judgment when he poked his head under a big stump and came out with his face full of porcupine quills.

I was a long ways from home so, after shooting the porky, I tied Buster into a knapsack with just his head sticking out and peddled my bicycle homeward like mad. I went directly to Fred's barbershop for help, knowing he would know exactly what to do.

Since there were so many quills, Fred gave my little dog a whiff of chloroform he had, thus putting him to sleep before beginning the task of pulling quills. I counted 113 before he was finished and probably missed some as they were not only in Buster's face but inside his throat and tongue. Without such thorough removal, the quills would likely have killed the little hound.

Midway of the removal work, though, Fred noticed my dog had quit breathing. Unruffled, he began giving the beagle artificial respiration by massaging the chest area. When the dog finally responded, Fred and I both heaved sighs of relief. Buster, by the way, never got close to another porcupine the rest of his days.

I have no idea where Fred got his knowledge of a dog's anatomy but he seemed well able to work with any kind of animals. Although he wasn't licensed to do so, people without much money often came to him with their female dogs and had them spayed in the back of his shop. That's probably why he kept a supply of chloroform on hand.

As a kid without a lot of money, either, I know Fred gave me a lot of breaks on the guns I bought from him every once in a while. (I still have a single-shot .22 Mossberg he let me have back then for $1.50.)

My first shotgun was a single-barrel 16-gauge that set me back $5. With just one chance to bag a bird or bunny, I credit that with really teaching me how to shoot and I got pretty good. But eventually, I decided I needed something with more firepower. I traded my shotgun in on a beautiful 16-gauge Fox Sterlingworth double with an $18 price tag on it.

I kept that gun for quite a while, even though it caused me quite a problem one time. Being thorough when I cleaned my guns, I opened up the mechanism to do the inside of the new one, too. Only thing, that's when a spring and several other parts came flying out.

After a long session of trying to fit those puzzle pieces together, I finally put all of the parts into a box and reluctantly took them over to Fred. He looked at them, shook his head, and said he would see what he could do when he got the time.

A couple days went by before he finally called me over to his shop. My shotgun, he said, was back in working order. He admitted finally he had worked on it nearly eight hours before getting everything back where it belonged.

Handing it to me, he said, "Don't EVER do that again!" Believe me — I didn't! Proving what a guy he was, when I apprehensively asked what I owed him for all of that work, he got a twinkle in his eye and replied, "Oh, I guess maybe 50 cents ought to be okay."

The last time I was visiting with Fred and talking about that and our other long-ago adventures, he finally admitted something. "You know, I think I sold you that shotgun too cheap!"

I had been thinking that for years but I sure as heck wasn't going to tell Fred Birdsey that!

Art Winnie always kept close track of the number
of days remaining before trout season opened.

ART WINNIE, FLY EXPERT

APPROACHING SPRINGTIME SOMETIMES caused me to pass up my regular haircuts near home and to take a hike downtown to Art Winnie's barbershop. Hanging in the front window of his shop was a huge wooden brook trout and below it were hung important numbers. Each day, Art would dutifully change the figures to let local fishermen know how many days remained before opening day of Michigan's trout season.

In my youthful enthusiasm, I was determined to not miss that very important day. Once in a while, I would even go in for a haircut. Between times, I would just drop by and watch in fascination as Art sat at his little workbench and whipped out the trout flies for which he was already becoming famous.

He confided in me that barbering was just something to do between times but he really did enjoy fly-fishing a lot more. Occasionally, he would give me a fly or two and I really appreciated that.

After all, it was just after the Great Depression and, like a lot of other people, I didn't have much money, least of all for trout flies. Art had to charge $2 for a dozen of his best flies and that was a lot of money in those times. Still, he managed to distribute thousands of them every year and even bought and paid cash for a $3,000 house that way.

Some years later, when Dr. James Hall moved to Traverse City and opened his medical practice, he had to attend a seminar in New York City. To kill a little time, he wandered into the famous Abercrombie & Fitch in that city and found the trout fishing section.

"I figured I should buy something there and picked out a dozen dry flies," he said. "I didn't want to bother carrying them around so I asked the clerk if they could be mailed to me and he said that would be fine. But when I gave him my name and address, he busted out laughing and told me I could have bought them cheaper in Traverse City. They had been tied by Art Winnie and shipped to New York!"

Art's reputation as a tyer of flies was so well-known that they could be found in all parts of the United States, Canada and even in such far-off countries as New Zealand and Australia.

Among his creations were the Michigan Hopper and the Caddis Fly. The latter fly became so famous that it still causes arguments to this day. His so-called "caddis" was really a giant mayfly, known better now to trout anglers as the "Hexagenia limbata" and has no resemblance to the actual caddis, which is something else again.

The Art Winnie term for the fly, though, was pretty much adopted by fishermen far and wide. That's how the big hatch which occurs on trout streams in late June and early July came to be known as "the caddis hatch." Some fishermen still call it that.

You might know that anybody who ties that many flies can't resist trying them on trout, too. Nearly any night during the big hatches, Art could be found on the Boardman River, whipping out his feathered creations with a split bamboo rod. There was never a doubt in anyone's mind that he could catch trout and he usually did.

By 1938, his exploits had become such that he was crowned

National Trout Festival King at Kalkaska, an honor which really boggled my young mind. After all, I regarded him with awe and that only strengthened that opinion.

The following year, I was equally impressed when Robinette Cornell, who lived just a few houses away from us on East Ninth Street, became National Trout Queen. Here I was, acquainted with two royal people! To my youthful mind, that was really something!

During my visits to Art Winnie's barbershop, I always managed to pick up some vital information about trout fishing. One thing fascinating me was his story about an enormous trout which inhabited the Boardman River and had repeatedly avoided capture by the area's best anglers, including Art himself.

Art called the trout "Big Chief" and said he thought it was a huge rainbow, although he never had it hooked long enough to prove that, so it could have been a big brown. The Boardman also had quite a few brook trout then but none ever got as big as Big Chief was reputed to be.

The hole where the whopper trout lived was a log jam across which a sunken barbed wire fence was also stretched. While rare to even get the trophy trout to take a fly, the battle always ended up the same way when the submerged fence or one of the logs would serve to snag and break the light leader required to fool Big Chief.

Maybe that big trout was just one of Art's yarns. I searched diligently for the location but never could find it. If I had, I had decided to forget all about flies. Instead, I would have drifted a nightcrawler or minnow into the log jam on a leader heavy enough to haul the whopper trout out and into my landing net.

But Art's enthusiasm for fly fishing rubbed off on me. When live bait failed to produce for me, I would often turn to either wet or dry flies. It sort of surprised me when such artificials worked and that knowledge led me to begin fly-tying on my own.

As a fumble-fingered kid, it was real intense work. I could manage maybe a half-dozen flies before I was so tensed up that I had to quit and go chop wood or something else physical to unwind. Even so, I turned out some great-looking (to me) creations.

Dry flies, with their hackles to make them float, were pretty much beyond my abilities, although I did turn out a few. Mostly, I concentrated on the easy nymphs which could be made with bright-colored thread from my mother's sewing box and peacock herl I picked up at the Clinch Park Zoo when those big birds would drop a feather.

Among my fondest memories was one evening when I got an early start to fish the waters below the old Keystone Dam. I had ridden my bicycle from town and waded cautiously into the river so as to not let water come over the tops of my hip boots. I had barely begun to fish when Art Winnie showed up and got into the river below me, dressed in his chest waders.

He always covered the water quickly with short, fast casts and soon overtook me and asked if I minded if he went by. Of course, I said I didn't mind. In fact, from then on, things worked out just fine. As I carefully waded upstream, whipping out one of my newly-created nymphs, something wonderful happened.

A nice brown trout inhaled the little fly and, after the normal fight, I netted the fish and slid it into my creel. Art grinned and waved and went on fishing. Shortly after, another brown took the same nymph, then another. After the third trout was creeled, though, Art was no longer smiling but had a serious look on his face as he waded back down to me.

"Hey, kid, what are you using?" the World's Greatest Trout Fisherman asked me. I nearly busted my shirt buttons as I brought my homemade fly out of the water and dangled it in front of him. It was a concoction that had just a bit of peacock herl wound around the front of the hook while the remainder consisted of only bright orange thread around the remainder of the hook shank.

"I've never seen anything like that," Art said as he looked it over closely. Admittedly, I hadn't either but the darned thing did catch fish for me that night. As for Art, I didn't see him land a trout that evening, a rarity, indeed. Imagine, I had just out-fished the world-famous Art Winnie! (That never happened again.)

One other time, however, I did get a high compliment from him. It happened after a heavy rain and I was up on the Boardman River fishing with nightcrawlers and doing pretty well. On my way back home, I stopped my bicycle near a culvert which ran under Cass Road and carried a tiny brook on into the river. The water had colored the stones there a bright orange, indicating its heavy iron content.

When I carefully floated the big worm down into the culvert I soon felt a throbbing which signalled a trout had taken the bait. When I set the hook all heck busted loose. What I knew was a heavy fish was thrashing wildly in the current and producing booming echoes from inside the metal pipe. Eventually, though, I was able to bring the trout out to where I could slide it into the nearby watercress and pounce on it.

Amazed at its size, I carefully measured it and found it was 21 inches long, plenty big enough for one of the coveted Che-Ge-Gon plaques then given out by the Traverse City Chamber of Commerce. I later weighed it as a 3.5-pounder and was so proud of it that I used my amateur taxidermy knowledge. That trout, by the way, still hangs on my wall at home.

What made this trout extra-special, however, was its coloration. After living in this one spot so long, the fish's skin had picked up the bright orange pigments of the iron water and was a brilliant orange, too. When I rode my bike into Traverse City, I immediately took it into Art Winnie's barbershop.

Ignoring its Che-Ge-Gon qualifications, he closely examined my fish. "That's the most beautiful brown trout I've ever seen!" said the World's Greatest Trout Fisherman.

The terrified visitor took the door right off the fish
shanty in his haste to leave.

HARRY DAY LOVED JOKES

OUR YOUTHFUL ENTHUSIASM for hunting and fishing probably caused Harry Day and me to become close friends back in the 1930s. He was a year older and much more' experienced in outdoor activities so I learned a lot from him.

When not attending classes at St. Francis High School in Traverse City, Harry worked for his father, Hank Day. Hank had a thriving business, something of a rarity then when much of the country was still digging out of the Great Depression era. It was "Day's Signs of All Kinds," located on East 12th Street. (Harry's son, Harry Jr., in fact, still runs the same business in the same location, as a third-generation owner.)

In addition to earning money from his father, Harry found extra advantages. One was getting to use Hank's car occasionally to head off to outdoor adventures.

Harry lost his driving privileges one springtime, though, when he drove to Beulah for the big smelt dip in Cold Creek. Taking several friends along for the exciting event, they really struck silver, so to speak.

The silvery little smelt were coming up out of Crystal Lake in heavy schools to spawn and for some reason there were fewer dippers than usual. In their excitement of hitting it so rich, they filled every container. Not wanting to abandon such a bonanza, and having a few forbidden drinks, Harry began to empty the buckets of still-wriggling smelt into the trunk of his father's car until that, too, was full.

Being midget fish and still alive, the smelt all flopped around. Some found their way into hidden crevices of the car trunk. They remained there long after the vehicle was unloaded back home.

The car trunk was full of fish slime and some of the missing smelt finally lost their sweet smell in the weeks ahead. It is easy to understand why Hank was more than a little disturbed with Harry.

Aside from banning Harry from using the car, Hank worked him harder than usual, as he rightly suspected some drinking had gone on, too. Instead of letting well enough alone, Harry the pedestrian managed to imbibe a bit too much on another occasion and that time Hank really fixed him.

Waking to a terrible hangover, Harry's head was pounding as he prepared to go to work on a hot, Saturday morning. As it went on, the day got even hotter. Hank had figured on that and ordered Harry to get up on a scaffold on the south side of the Wilson Furniture building and paint the entire wall where a new sign was to be displayed.

"I was sure I was going to doe!" Harry confided in me a little later. "Dad sure did know how to make a point!" After that, he pretty much decided drinking just wasn't worth it.

Harry was also able to create new excitement out of winter fishing for smelt on Crystal Lake, once he got to use Hank's car again. Along with Tom Donley and Dick Weiler (who later became sheriff in Grand Traverse County), Harry owned a spacious smelt fishing shanty on the lake.

The trio called themselves "Tom, Dick and Harry," a rather logical reference.

They always held a contest whereby the first one to hook a

smelt had to bring it up into the shanty and bite its head off. There was plenty of evasion but sooner or later somebody was forced to admit having a smelt on the line, then the really serious fishing could begin.

One night a rather timid visitor came by to see how Tom, Dick and Harry were doing. Harry immediately sensed the opportunity for one of his practical jokes and began to work on the guy.

He started grumbling about the oil heater being faulty and mentioned that a fuel buildup would occasionally make the stove explode. "That's when we have to get out of here — fast!" he emphasized. Meanwhile, he had quietly reached over and put a whistling tea kettle on top of the little stove.

Eventually, as he kept dropping other dire hints and the visitor's nerves got more ragged, Harry's dire plot bore fruit. The tea kettle let out with a low screech which quickly became louder. "There she goes now!" Harry yelled.

He had hardly opened his mouth, though, before the terrified visitor whirled from his seat and, without even trying to unhook it, took the shanty door right off its hinges as he plunged out into the night!

After the laughing had died down, though, the trio of pranksters were faced with the task of somehow replacing the mangled fish coop door.

On another occasion, Harry and I were ice fishing for perch and ciscoes in West Grand Traverse Bay, just off the old We-Que-Tong Yacht Club building. (Near where the Holiday Inn sits now.) It was a cold but clear day and the ice was still freezing, as was obvious from the occasional, natural rumbling and accompanying pressure cracks.

The ice was fairly well crowded with other fishing hopefuls, all bundled up against the cold. We were somewhat surprised to finally look up and see two men approaching gingerly. We guessed from their top coats, suits and street shoes they were probably salesmen who had likely stayed overnight at the Park Place Hotel.

Biting fish distracted us for several minutes, then we heard some light chipping on the ice nearby. One of the strangers was down on his hands and knees, trying to cut a hole in the ice with a pocket knife blade.

Figuring that would take them forever, Harry walked over and handed them our ice spud, suggesting that would be a lot faster and easier.

As he walked away from the grateful fishermen, however, Harry couldn't resist a tongue-in-cheek warning: "Be careful how you use that thing. If you hit the ice too hard the vibrations could break up all of the ice out here on the bay!"

Paying heed, the would-be angler gingerly pecked a little while with the ice chisel, then gradually pounded harder as the chips flew. Before he hit water, though, one of the loudest rumbles and pressure cracks ran across the bay as temperatures dropped a bit more.

"Now look what you done!" yelled Harry. The wide-eyed salesmen didn't stop to look back. Dropping the spud where it was, the two of them took off running for the safety of shore, slipping and sliding as they went.

Harry and I, along with other nearby fishermen, nearly went into hysterics. But eventually we recovered enough to go on catching perch and ciscoes despite the continuing booming freeze noises.

Hip boots are supposed to stay dry inside but,
somehow, that rarely happened.

HIP BOOTS NEVER GOT DRY

HIP BOOTS ARE supposed to be dry inside and only get wet on the outside. That, at least, is the general idea.

It didn't always work that way with Dad's black rubber hip boots which somehow always seemed to be just as wet inside as they were on the outer layer. Dad commented on this oddity every time he pulled on his boots and found them still wet inside. Leaking had nothing to do with it.

When Dad moved our family from Ohio to Traverse City in the 1930s, the Great Depression was still making its effects felt and money for everything was just plain tight. Economics figured into everything so when Dad decided he needed the boots to use for fishing or hunting, we ended up with only one pair.

I could understand that but when the great outdoors beckoned to me and I knew Dad was working or couldn't go out for some other reason, I had no qualms about borrowing his hip boots. They were a lot larger than I needed but by pulling on three pairs of heavy wool socks, my feet didn't slip around in them too much. It could have had something to do, though, with what appeared to be clumsiness on my part.

A kid in oversize hip boots is bound to make a few mis-steps, at least once in a while. I tended to make a career of it, though.

Maybe I should have taken notes in those early years. If there is such a thing as a record for the number of times and places to fill hip boots with water, my name might today be in some record book.

Mostly, this seemed to happen when I was trying to stay dry while hunting ducks. Putting out decoys in the shallows is best done by wading, to make sure they are in the proper formations to attract the real thing. I was fairly successful at that but, due to the many opportunities, I always managed to wade in over the tops of the boots.

Dad's boots, therefore, were properly baptized in such widespread locations as the Lake Leelanau marsh and all of the impoundments of the Boardman River south of Traverse City. There were also several potholes located in nearby woodlands where I managed to get wet. It was no problem at all to go over the tops when wading the cattail growths which were then so abundant along the shorelines of both East and West Grand Traverse Bays. I slurped them all into Dad's boots!

Autumn waters are always cold but summer trout streams are no bargain, either. I gave his boots equal treatment during the so-called "warm weather" months. That was usually more often, too, since I was out of school then but Dad had to work nearly every day at the Grand Traverse Metal Casket Company.

Wading just about anywhere in the Boardman River was a near-guarantee that I was going to get wet, along with the insides of Dad's boots. The swift-flowing current, combined with slippery rocks and the uncertainty of perhaps stepping into a hidden hole or tripping over an unseen log underwater, virtually assured success in wetness.

But when it came to a generally shallow stream like Platte River, a little ingenuity was required. Most of that little stream had very clear water and was full of small gravel, instead of

Boardman-size rocks. You could see underwater obstacles long before you might trip over them, which sort of spoiled things for anybody intending to get wet inside and out.

I still can remember, with a touch of pride, the spectacular exhibition I put on one day on the Platte when Fred Swaney and I were camping near Clark's Mill. Climbing out of the tent early and determined to beat Fred to the best fishing hole in the area one morning, I quickly pulled on the boots, leaving them rolled down for easier walking.

They were still that way when I approached the old mill and started to make my way across a narrow board walk which was constantly being splashed by water. Such activity had also given it a sort of mossy slickness, although I was unaware of that right then. That rapidly changed, though, about midway of the walkway and I went into a fantastic skid. Fred emerged from our tent just in time to see the entire performance and later admitted that he was downright "amazed" at my gymnastics.

Slipping and sliding and waving both arms in what must have been graceful motions, I made it barely past the middle of the walkway before losing my balance. Crashing down onto the boards and one of the pilings supporting the walk, I sort of rolled off in slow motion before disappearing under the water. When I came back up, shocked into faster action by the cold water, Fred had run up to the bank.

Instead of applauding, though, he had the nerve to laugh! Having the breath knocked out of me, I couldn't immediately comment on that for' a few minutes, then decided some dry clothes might be in order. The boots, obviously, were as full of water as I had ever seen them, even in a rolled-down style.

Sure, I know, anybody can get wet in a river or lake but it takes something extra to accomplish that in a little creek. Few places in the Asylum Creek were deep enough to fill hip boots and Mitchell Creek wasn't much improvement in that regard.

I did show Fred how on Mitchell Creek one day, though.

Being somewhat proud of my jumping abilities, I bet Fred I could jump from one bank to the other, despite wearing Dad's hip boots. He laughed and said I couldn't, which was challenge enough. Getting back for a running start, I took off in a magnificent leap which did take me to the other side. Only thing, I didn't realize the sod there had been undercut by the creek current and as I landed, it began to crumble.

In panic, I leaned forward and grabbed a double handful of grass and hung on. Sort of in slow-motion, the grass pulled out of the ground, leaving me with nowhere to go but flat on my back in the middle of the creek. The boots, of course, filled with water but that was the least of it.

Probably my finest hour at getting wet, however, came on a tiny brook which could have been little more than a foot wide but relatively deep. Brook trout lurked in its depths and grabbed worms which were floated to them on the current.

This day, I cautiously approached a little waterfall which dropped nearly three feet into a dark pool below. After snaking a fat brookie out, I approached a little closer to see if there might be a continuing pool downstream.

Clay is always wet and slippery and there was some there, hidden and waiting. As one boot foot encountered it, the other one followed. I skidded neatly over the edge and into the pool. The merry little waterfall completed things by pouring a full quota of water into the top of the hip boots, nearly filling them before I could scramble out. Talk about spectacular!

Expensive or not, Dad finally got tired of finding his boots always wet inside. That's how it happened the second Christmas we spent in Traverse City, a box under the tree contained — you guessed it — my very own pair of hip boots.

Came opening day of the next trout season and I was in those new hip boots and checking out one of the local creeks. But somehow, I had forgotten about the old barbed wire fence strand buried in the grass.

The tear it made wasn't all that big and I was able to get a patch vulcanized on at one of the gas stations in the Old Town neighborhood. That almost did the job, except for a slight leak — enough to remind me that fishing in wet hip boots isn't really all that bad, anyhow.

THE HUNTING WAS GREAT

A S A TRANSPLANTED teenager from Ohio, I considered myself a sort of Daniel Boone-type when we moved to the wilds of the Traverse City area in the 1930s. Maybe nobody else thought of this as wilderness back then but, compared to what it has become these days, that wasn't a bad assumption for a kid to make. Although my only transportaion was my bicycle, I managed to explore in every direction.

When the fall hunting seasons opened, I spent every opportunity looking for small game with my shotgun. That even included the few remaining hours after school before daylight failed and nearly fulltime on weekends, except when Mom and Dad insisted I go to church with them and my sister.

Ruffed grouse were abundant nearly everywhere, even though hardly anybody called them that. Instead, they were referred to as partridge or "pats" for short. Dad hardly talked about them at all, vowing they were so close to being impossible to hit that he wouldn't even shoot at them as they thundered away to safety.

I looked upon them as a challenge, though, and vowed to become an expert on pats. Little did I know, however, what I had promised myself although by season-end, I did have a rough idea. That came about due to the idea that it would help if I kept accurate records. The result was extremely humbling.

During that first fall of hunting I managed to kill only three of those elusive birds. I was downright amazed to find, though, that I had blown 42 of my precious 16-gauge shells to do so. Actually, my average would have been even worse if I hadn't caught one pat in a hemlock tree during an early snow and blasted him off the branch.

Nobody told me that you don't do such things to such magnificient gamebirds. But since my mind then was on using hunting as an extra method of putting food on the table I didn't really see anything wrong with it then.

By the time the next hunting season came around, I had decided to be more selective and not shoot at every pat which blasted out of cover ahead of me. I found, for example, that by hunting on rainy days, the birds were a little slower in getting airborne, which gave me extra precious time to swing on them. I also quit trying to shoot through trees after the thunderbirds had left. My averages improved, although I still manage to miss my share of all kinds of gamebirds, even after all of these years.

Using my bicycle and carrying my little beagle, Buster, in the basket, I frequently wandered up into Leelanau County to search for partridge, cottontails or just about anything else in the way of small game. That's how I happened to be working my way along near Brewery Creek when something marvelous happened.

Wild grapes were growing there and stretching far off the ground into some of the trees. As I approached, a brilliantly-clad, long-tailed bird suddenly exploded into flight. When that big cock pheasant rose into the air cackling, I very nearly failed to respond.

Luckily for me, however, he had problems getting completely free from the tangle of vines and I was able to get off a quick shot with my single barrel. When he came crashing down, I rushed to grab what I believed must be the most beautiful bird in the world.

A little later that same year, Buster and I were investigating a weedy swale along M-72, near what is now a big shopping complex and a string of houses. My little hound flushed a rooster ringneck and I was happy to see that one drop when I shot. Less than an hour later, in the same area, we were checking out a nearby grape vineyard and another rooster made the mistake of getting up in easy range.

With two pheasants bagged, I found myself in the unusual position of having to quit hunting the long-tailed birds that day since two was the daily limit!

Actually, there were more pheasants around the Traverse City area back then than most people believed, although not really enough to hunt for them exclusively. Most of the ringnecks we encountered were found while we were looking for something else.

Due to a general lack of hunting, some of those pheasants must have eventually died of old age. One that didn't, though, was dropped by Fred Swaney while we were hunting some swales up behind the Concrete Service facility out West Front Street.

That magnificent trophy bird was heavy and had inch-long spurs, indicating it was an old rooster. It had an overall length of 42 inches, beak to tail end, and was the biggest ringneck I have ever seen, right up to now. Fred was so proud of that cock bird that he used his amateur taxidermy skills to mount it and kept it in his bedroom at home for years.

While most of the land in the Traverse City area was privately owned, nobody really cared if kids or adults used it for hunting. I took full advantage of that and hunted off in all directions, although I seemed to have a preference for the woods and swales and brush found to the west of town.

Buster was nearly always with me on our various hunting expeditions and occasionally it paid off for me in surprising ways. I often ended up with a mixed bag of wildlife, most of which went onto the table after Mom prepared it with one of her many recipes.

Probably the most memorable day of that type came the morning he flushed a ringneck rooster for me and I dropped it. I had hardly tucked it into the game pocket of my hunting coat when a partridge came roaring past, right out in the open and I dumped that bird, too. The little dog next poked his curious nose into a thicket where a woodcock was resting. I added that bird to my collection, too.

During the remainder of that hunt, which went well past noon, Buster jumped two cottontails, both of which I rolled, then put a big fox squirrel up a tree. By then my rear end was pretty well dragging with all of that unplanned weight in the back of my hunting jacket.

I decided then to hike back to where my bicycle was concealed in some brush and took a short cut through a patch of hardwoods. When Buster began to bark in his usual frantic manner, I fully expected another cottontail to come my way.

As I stood waiting on the wooded ridge, though, I was rather shocked to see a red fox headed directly for me. My 16-gauge single-shot was loaded with No. 6 pellets and there was no time to change to anything heavier so I just stood my ground.

Finally, when the fox was only about 25 yards away, I pulled up quickly and fired, hitting him in the face and killing him instantly. The pelt would have been worth slightly more later in the season but I was still willing to haul the extra load of the fox the remaining distance to my bicycle for the peddle on home.

In the 1930s, fur prices left a lot to be desired. A pretty good fox might bring as little as $1.50 but it all added up and when I could manage to shoot one ahead of Buster, I did just that.

One season I collected four of them while rabbit hunting.

During the off-seasons, Fred Swaney and I often did some extra hunting just to keep our shooting eyes sharp. Crows were especially fun to fool, although at times that seemed to work the other way around. In the springtime, however, the black rascals seemed a little bit easier to call within range of our shotguns.

Our methods were simple — just find a spot where we knew crows were likely to fly by in early morning or on the way back to roost at night. Concealing ourselves in a clump of cedar, when possible, we found we were able to call the birds in close.

Not wanting to spend our meager funds on artificial calls, we learned we could "talk crow" with just our mouths. At least, the crows thought that's what it was and quite a few fell to our scattergunning.

Plinking with a .22 rifle also helped our skills with those guns and made it easier later on to collect squirrels which were legal each autumn. Between times, we found another, much more challenging live target.

Riding our bikes out over the rough gravel which was then Hammond Road, we came one day to the Sleder farm. (Where the Elmwood Golf Course is located now.) Noticing lots of pigeons flying in and out of a silo alongside the barn, we stopped there to check it out.

Mr. Sleder agreed that the pigeons were a downright nuisance, messy and he said he wouldn't mind it if we wanted to help thin them out with our .22s.

"Just be sure you don't shoot any holes in the barn roof or the silo," he warned. Fred and I agreed we would be careful and upheld our part of that bargain.

Luckily, none of that area was too well populated then because our aim was often nearly straight up when we could find a pigeon peeking over the edge. Where our .22 slugs might have come down was something we didn't even consider then but it would be highly dangerous now.

The first pigeons we shot were fairly easy but they learned fast and the opportunities began to dwindle. We had to hide and avoid moving around until the flocks had returned to their lofty perches on the buildings.

Even when a domestic pigeon is shot right through the chest, it still has a lot of stamina and is able to fly some distance before dropping dead. We retrieved all of our birds, though, and took them home for table fare. Mom had read somewhere about "squab under glass" and created some fine food from the pigeons we brought back from our off-season hunts.

After the first few times of stopping in to ask permission before beginning our pigeon hunting, Fred and I sort of goofed up one spring morning. We just parked our bikes out by the road, then walked directly into the barn and silo area and began popping away with our .22 rifles.

Suddenly, a guy we had never seen before came roaring out of the house and yelling. He was so mad we decided it would be futile to even try to explain that our hunts had been approved by old Mr. Sleder himself. Instead, the two of us just fled at full speed back to our bikes, hopped onto them and peddled like mad away from there.

We were so scared that we never did go back, either. Still, it did have one virtue. Ever since then, I like to ask ahead of time when I intend to hunt on private property. Knowing it is okay leaves you with a really fine and secure feeling.

Picking nightcrawlers on the Asylum Grounds was
spooky enough without somebody sneaking up
in the dark.

FISHING BAITS TOOK EFFORT

THERE'S A NICE little office building sitting on the shore of West Grand Traverse Bay right where M-72 runs into M-22. I'll bet nobody working there has any idea that they are walking around on top of a valuable pile of copper.

Back in the late 1930s, the late Lud Garthe owned a strip of land there but it was too small to build on. He was also part-owner of the Grand Traverse Metal Casket Company which overlooked Boardman Lake. Those fancy burial boxes were often made of solid sheet copper so they would last a long time.

Manufacturing, however, resulted in a lot of scrap copper and a disposal problem. Lud solved that by having some steel pilings driven into the water of the bay, far enough from shore that he could fill in a big lot behind it. Into that spot went all kinds of copper and other casket debris until it eventually filled up. Then over it all, dirt was dumped and smoothed off and he had a nice building lot, practically free. (That was legal back in those days or at least nobody challenged it like they do nowadays when somebody wants to fill in bottomlands.)

Fred Swaney and I were then kids in high school and since our fathers worked at the casket company we knew all about the scrap copper. One day it dawned on us that here was a wonderful source of homemade fishing lures. We didn't have much money in those days following the Great Depression so we had to make do with whatever we could find. That's how we came to get into recycling, although nobody called it by that term then.

Back in my basement, we laboriously cut out spoon shapes with heavy tin snips, then pounded them into rough lures. Lacking split rings, which cost money, we used light wire, looped around twice, to fasten treble hooks to each one through a drilled hole. Fishing lines went through the other ends of each spoon.

Pedaling our bicycles to the Boardman River, we first tried our new killer lures in the area just south of Eighth Street where the old Oval Wood Dish Company had been located. There was still a boom there holding floating logs and we figured there should be northern pike near such cover.

Our first casts didn't produce much when retrieved at normal speeds so we began to let the spoons drop lower, toward bottom. That made us lose a couple of them on snags. Considering the work that went into them we should have felt bad but since the spoons were "free" it wasn't really too serious. We had to quit losing them, though.

When my spoon went to bottom as I was working a backlash out of my casting reel, I finally began to crank it in as fast as I could. The result was a smashing strike and I was fast to a mad northern that I soon landed. That gave me an idea, so on the next cast I again reeled in as fast as possible and hooked another pike. Obviously, there was no way we could retrieve so rapidly that a pike couldn't catch the lure. In fact, the moving spoon must have looked like a small bait fish trying to escape and the pike went after it before that could happen.

Fred and I both continued to reel in as fast as we could and in a very short time we had our five-fish limits of scrappy northerns. I have used that same technique a number of times since and it still works on pike today, especially when they seem reluctant to strike a lure.

Although the Oval Wood Dish Company had ceased its operations by then, some rather dangerous things were left behind. The boomed logs, for example, were inviting to a couple of kids seeking adventure. I got to wondering how far out on them I could walk and one day gave it a try. I hadn't gone very far before I found the floating logs tended to turn over slowly if you didn't balance yourself just right.

My balance wasn't all that great but somehow I managed to stay on top of each one before jumping to another, which also began to roll over. There was every chance that I would eventually slip and fall in between some of the giant logs and, not being much of a swimmer... well, I was definitely not going to let that happen if I could possibly prevent it.

I just kept hopping and jumping and finally got turned around to where I ingloriously fled for shore, vowing to never get into a spot like that again. I was definitely not the lumber-jack type who could balance easily on a rolling log! I decided to leave that to some of my book heroes.

But, I thought Fred got into an even dumber kind of predicament. The company had also put up an old water tower on the east bank of the river. It was long unused but had an iron ladder running up to the top of it. Fred got to wondering how the view might be from up there and decided to climb it one day. I bowed out of that one as such high places bothered me. Instead, I sat down on the ground and watched Fred climb the rickety rungs of the ladder.

Just before he got to the top, he noticed some of the rusty bolts holding the ladder were beginning to pull loose from the wooden portion of the old water tank. He quickly scrambled on up to the top of the tower, shaken by his discovery, then wondered how he could ever get back down.

He must have sat up there for an hour or more, trying to figure a way out of his problem. I was certainly no help and was sure that if he tried to come down, the bolts would pull loose and Fred, ladder and all, would arrive on the ground in a heap. It was a frightening thought but I wondered how I might go about explaining that to his mom and dad .

It was getting near dark when Fred finally decided he had to do something if he didn't want to spend the night up there. Had he tried that he might have rolled off, anyhow, in his sleep, providing he ever did get to sleep.

He finally screwed up his courage enough to again reach a foot over and lightly touch the old ladder. That much accomplished, he got his other foot onto the same rung. It held so he gingerly put more weight on and gradually and slowly came down the ladder. The bolts remained at least partly holding in the rotting wood, even if they did groan as he climbed down.

I understood completely when Fred jumped the last ten feet to safety, then bent down and kissed the ground. When I asked if he had been real scared, he shook his head. "Naw, it wasn't that bad. You should just see the view from up there." I decided to just take his word for that.

That part of the Boardman River banks today has filled up full of "civilization" of sorts. Where the old Oval Wood Dish Company and its water tower once sat is an office complex now. On the opposite side of the river is a row of condominiums whose occupants can't possibly imagine the outdoor adventures which took place there a half-century ago.

Although our homemade copper spoons were fine for northern pike and even an occasional, oversize smallmouth bass, the really reliable fishing bait was worms. We had places where the black muck was always moist and worms could be dug, even if it was a lot of work. Picking up nightcrawlers was more interesting and our young backs held up well under such after-dark activity, which often took hours.

Fred and I used to pedal our bikes over to the Asylum Grounds which had large, spacious lawns that were always neatly mowed and clipped by some of the better mental patients who enjoyed keeping busy. It was, admittedly, a spooky place after dark because you always wondered if one of the really dangerous patients might have escaped and was wandering around in the black of night.

When we went there together, though, Fred and I kept tabs on one another by our flashlights which we kept as dim as possible and close to the ground. That was done in order to not alarm the big nightcrawlers. Most kept their tail ends anchored in a hole in the ground and when disturbed could whip back fast. It often left us wondering if there had even been a big worm there in the first place.

Sneaky individuals catch the most nightcrawlers, too, as vibrations from a heavy-footed hunter could send the big worms into their security holes in a hurry. Knowing that, we sneaked up on our prey, ever so carefully. The flashlight beam was shined off to one side when we spotted one of the worms. We would then grab it firmly, yet not so tight as to break it in two.

Finally, when the pressure didn't let up, the crawler would relax just enough to get a better hold and could be pulled the rest of the way out of the ground and dropped into the bait bucket.

We often gathered a couple hundred of the giant worms in a single night, thus obtaining fine fishing bait to use on bass, trout and some of the bigger panfish. The fish we caught were always taken home and were a very important food source in those cash-poor times.

One night after a daylong downpour, it had finally quit raining and I decided it was perfect for nightcrawler hunting. Fred wasn't home when I phoned so I went alone to the Asylum Grounds on my bicycle, figuring I could really make a big haul of nightcrawlers. I was right, too, because worms of all sizes were everywhere, many not even anchored in their burrows.

It was an especially dark night, too, with heavy clouds left over from the day of rain. That made it a little eerie as I gradually worked my way along the wet, green lawns and kept filling my bait container.

Sound was carrying a little too well, though, and I couldn't help but listen to some of the mental patients shrieking from behind the barred windows of nearby buildings.

One in particular left her message imbedded in my memory, even today, as she yelled repeatedly: "Great big bodies rolling down the river!" That was followed by crazy laughter that had the hair on the back of my neck crawling. I tried to ignore it and kept on hunting the big worms.

Fred, meanwhile, had come home, then checked over at my house where Mom told him I had gone nightcrawler hunting. He pedaled his bike to our regular grounds and saw my little light working across the lawns.

The first I realized I was no longer alone was when he crept silently up behind me, grabbed me around the waist and yelled: "I gotcha!"

If there was ever an Olympic event dealing with the tossing of a bait bucket, I would have won it right there. It took me minutes to get my breath back, even after I realized it was only Fred and not one of the violent mental patients I imagined might be around.

Only after he helped me locate my bait pail and to pick up some of the piles of writhing nightcrawlers did I forgive him. I guess there is more than one way to prove just how strong your heart really is.

ASYLUM CREEK REALLY CHANGED

BECAUSE IT WAS so close, one of Dad's favorite trout streams was the Asylum Creek. That's what it was called in the 1930s and for quite a while after until some thought it should undergo a name change to remove a "stigma."

With Dad doing the pedaling and me riding the crossbars of my bicycle, we often visited it together. As is the case now, the creek began its journey in a number of tiny tributary brooks in the hills south of Traverse City. They eventually joined the main creek which, in turn, is a Boardman River branch that ends in West Grand Traverse Bay .

During those early years, Dad and I must have fished every foot of the Asylum Creek, from its mouth on up to the top of every branch with enough water in it to hold a trout. The upper reaches contained nothing but brook trout which were Dad's favorite, although a few brown trout were then beginning to show up, along with a number of rainbows.

A day was considered an outstanding success whenever Dad would manage to fill his willow creel with a limit of 15 nice brook trout. He didn't believe in wasting anything but distained browns and rainbows as "foreign fish" not worth keeping and tossed them back. When one of them was hooked too deeply, though, and was obviously going to die, he would take it back home to feed to the cat.

Generally, we fished the creek on our hands and knees, crawling carefully up to the stream so the trout would have no idea danger was close. That still works, since trout are as spooky as ever and refuse to bite once they see you or your shadow.

Only once can I remember carelessness paying off. Dad was in a hurry to reach a pool just upstream and splashed through the creek to reach the other side from where the offering of his worm-baited hook would be better. As he hit the stream, a rainbow of about 20 inches, became startled and swam right up onto a gravel bar.

Dad quickly reached down and grabbed it. Holding it for me to see, he stuffed it into his open creel, then locked the lid back down. "It's only a rainbow," he said, "but God must have wanted me to have it." (The cat didn't get that one.)

Although he fished hard and often, Dad never did achieve one goal. He always wanted to catch a brook trout at least 12 inches long. In fact, he had a foot-long ruler wired to the top of his creel, just waiting for the day that occasion might arrive. The best he could do was 11.5 inches — close but not quite what he was seeking. The remainder of our Asylum Creek brookies ranged on down to bare keepers of seven inches.

Brook trout from the clear, clean waters of the Asylum Creek were wonderful on the table, too. Many a day, when Dad was working and I was free for the summer, I would pay a visit to the stream and get home just in time for lunch. Mom would fry up a few of the brookies, then we would carefully remove the skeleton to eliminate every bone. The two cooked fillets would go hot onto a slice of butter bread for some of the best taste treats imaginable. Equally important in those days of short finances, it was nearly free!

The Asylum Creek was so-named because a long portion of

it flowed through the grounds of the Traverse City Insane Asylum. At one time, its many picturesque buildings housed close to 2,000 patients and employment was provided for a good many Traverse City residents. The grounds had huge barns with prize-winning cattle and patients who were able to do so worked in the farm fields as surprisingly helpful therapy.

Eventually, though, some of the state unions pressured for elimination of the self-help farming so all food had to be purchased from downstate afterwards. It wasn't long after, either, that a name change was forced and the facility came to be known as the Traverse City State Hospital. That change carried over to the little stream which was then called "Hospital Creek," Dad, however, kept right on referring to it as the Asylum Creek, as did most others.

It was Omer Curtis, then a public relations official for the mental hospital, who later obtained an official change in the creek's name. Figuring it would be good publicity and good for local boys and girls, he convinced the City Commission to change it to "Kids Creek."

That opened the way for an annual fishing contest under State Hospital sponsorship in which kids under 14 fished the creek and won a number of prizes donated by area merchants. After Curtis retired and moved away, the local chapter of Trout Unlimited took over the contest but they, too, eventually tired of the work involved.

A few signs were erected on the hospital grounds to indicate the section inside the city limits was reserved for kids. South of 14th Street and the Silver Lake Road, though, there were never any such restrictions as that is in Garfield Township. Besides, for many years that was all wild, open land with few buildings. Little did Dad and I dream how all of that would someday change when we fished there in the 1930s and early 1940s!

One of the first intrusions of civilization came just west of

Franke Road when a new subdivision was built on the site of what was once a huge pig farm. When drainage proved so poor that raw sewage was flowing into the creek tributaries, area residents began referring to it as "Piggyville." Eventually, it became so bad that it had to be linked up with the Traverse City sewage system, even though it was outside of the city.

Other buildings began to appear on soil that was equally poor for drainage and septic absorption, including the black muck area where an old mill pond had once stood. Such continuing assaults on the Asylum Creek continued until the artificial run-off from roofs, lawns and huge paved parking lots made every rainfall a hazard. More than once the little stream aimed such a torrent of water into the city that Cedar Street, just south of Front Street, became a flooding pond. This, as much as anything, finally forced formation of groups opposed to all further building on the creek's flood plain. Their success has been limited.

That, however, only came about recently — much too late to prevent the entire area along US-31 south of Traverse City from become a congested jumble of commercial business sites. When it got in the way, early developers just ran the Asylum Creek underground through long culverts. Portions of its branches are thus buried throughout much of Traverse City today.

As for the Asylum Grounds themselves, they appear to be undergoing kinder treatment. Due to the presence of the Asylum Creek and huge expanses of what were once the black muck farmlands, much of it is not suitable for building and restrictions on that are firmly in place today.

When the State of Michigan finally closed the Traverse City State Hospital a few years ago, developers licked their chops at the possibilities there. During that same general period, the most picturesque of the castlelike buildings were in mortal danger but hardly anybody knew it.

By an odd twist of fate, I was heading for a Canadian fishing trip with some area friends and riding with Paul Guthrie who owned an earth-moving business in the Mesick area. Enroute, he happened to mention that he had lost out on a bid to demolish some of the State Hospital buildings.

The very first thing I did on returning to Traverse City was to inform the editors of the Record-Eagle who had also been unaware of the impending threat to the wonderful old buildings. The paper launched an investigation, got area lawmakers involved and were barely in time to stop the wrecking balls which had already been moved onto the state site.

Eventually, the City of Traverse City succeeded in buying the majority of the old Asylum Grounds for $1. A new corporation was formed and called "Grand Traverse Commons." It will preserve the majority of the former mental hospital grounds as a park, since much of it has grown up into at least partial woodlands.

The old buildings will be mostly preserved as historic sites and remodeled to provide senior housing and other citizen services. Part will be used by Munson Medical Center, which has constantly overflowed its capacity and desperately needs the space, including more parking.

Much of the lawn areas, where Fred Swaney and I once picked nightcrawlers in the 1930s, have already been turned into black-top for parking and others will soon follow. Still, it could have been a lot worse.

Through it all, though, the old Asylum Creek still flows, sometimes with a lot more volume than the folks on South Cedar Street appreciate. Farther south, in Garfield Township, building continues with new malls and other structures with heavy runoff after every rain.

Bob Drake, one of my 1939 classmates, has plenty of reason to miss the "good old days." When he built his home on what has now become South Airport Road, it overlooked in the back an area where his father had once taken part in a rousing bear hunt. Scenic and wild, Bob figured it would always remain that way. It didn't.

Faced with the huge Grand Traverse Mall, directly across from his home, he eventually decided he could no longer fight the advances of civilization. He sold out and moved in 1993 and his longtime home was quickly moved and the yard bulldozed to make way for more commercial development.

Change is inevitable, of course. But when I think of the Traverse City of the late 1930s and compare it with what it is becoming toddy, I have to admit I don't like what I'm seeing. I don't think Dad would have, either.

Being bombed by falling cows was only one of
the hazards of fishing on the Boardman River at
night.

NIGHT FISHING ADVENTURES

NIGHT FISHING ON a darkened trout stream is usually a quiet adventure.

Under normal conditions the only sound is the gentle "swish, swish" of a flyline as it unwinds to carry the fly toward hoped-for waiting trout. Occasionally, it will blend in with the thrumming call of a nighthawk or perhaps a whippoorwill.

From the time I first began to fish the Boardman River, back in the 1930s, this has not always held true. Relaxation sometimes became something else altogether, particularly in the vicinity of the old Keystone Dam south of Traverse City.

As a kid then, I often peddled my bicycle to the dam in early evening, especially when what Art Winnie called "the caddis hatch" was coming on. The backwater above the dam could generally be counted on to produce a good hatch and get some pretty good brown trout feeding. That's what I had in mind one night as I stood in the water close to the tops of my hip boots.

Carefully laying out a fly into the semi-darkness, I finally noticed a muskrat swimming along. Figuring the animal might hit my flyline, I quickly lifted the flyrod. My timing was off slightly, however, and my fly hooked the muskrat right in the back.

There was a terrific explosion as the startled animal suddenly submerged, then began to take out line toward the far side of the little pond. The action didn't end until the muskrat had obviously made it to the relative safety of its den burrow in the opposite river bank and the leader broke.

I was left to wonder how the furbearer might explain its new ornament to other muskrats it might happen to meet.

Another night I had waded out into the pond shallows as far as possible to begin casting my fly. Again, all was quiet and peaceful as I stood there casting alone and enjoying the peaceful silence.

Beavers have a way of moving through the water almost silently and I had no way of realizing one was swimming past right behind me. The first hint I had was when I made another cast, the beaver saw the movement and gave a resounding slap with its tail on the water's surface.

That close, it was like a gun going off as the big animal vanished underwater in a splashing dive. Something like that is a dandy way to check out the condition of your heart. Obviously, I survived that unplanned test!

My sometimes-fishing partner, Fred Swaney, one night saw a big watersnake swimming across Keystone Pond and, on a whim, decided to see if he could hook it. He did, then was faced with the problem of wondering how to unhook it. Watersnakes are not poisonous but can give you a nasty bite so Fred eventually decided it wasn't worth while to try saving his fly imbedded in the snake's middle. He purposely broke the leader, leaving the angry reptile to swim away with one of his best flies.

Even good night fishermen often get skunked — meaning they don't catch anything. One father-and-son team, though, nearly had the real thing in the Keystone area. The boy, about 15, was casting a fly into the darkness when he felt a mighty tug and was fast to something. He figured it had to be a big brown trout and called his father over to help net it.

The "fish," however, turned out to be a very lively skunk that had apparently been swimming to get across the river when the fly landed on its back and dug in. The lad and his dad were both mighty relieved when the light leader and skunk were able to go their separate ways — without retaliation by the animal.

The late Dr. Jim Hall's favorite fly fishing spot on the Boardman River used to be below the Keystone Dam area where there is a very high bank. Jim liked to tell of a friend who was fishing there one black night and enjoying the peace and quiet while swishing his fly out into the darkness. As he did so, he was unaware of what was going on atop the steep bank behind him.

A herd of cows fed contentedly up there on the lush grass which grew right to the edge of the bluff. One, likely reaching just a little too far for a choice mouthful, slipped and went over the edge.

Down she came, crashing into the water and barely missing the unsuspecting angler. Before he could begin to recover from the shock, the cow scrambled out of the river and headed upstream to a spot where she could get back up into the pasture.

Finally regaining his composure and after letting his fishing spot rest a short time, the fisherman shrugged off the aerial assault and went back to his task of laying out a dry fly once more.

How could he know that "history would repeat" and a second Jersey would bounce down the bluff and, again, land in the river. This time, the distance between cow and angler was even closer. That's when he decided to quit tempting fate and deserted his favorite fishing spot for all time.

He told his harrowing tale to Jim Hall the next day, whereupon Jim also decided that the possibility of being bombed by a cow was not worth the risk of fishing in that spot, either. As far as I know, Jim never returned to his favorite brown trout hole below the bluff, not even during the height of the caddis hatch.

Something like that tends to leave an impression on a guy, even when heard second-hand. I'll admit that I only fished that choice location just once after hearing the tale. But even that wasn't until after I had first checked out the top of the bluff to make sure there were no cattle grazing up there. Still, it was with a nervous feeling to be uncertain if those cows might happen to sneak into that section of pasture while I was busy trying to entice a trout to my fly.

Today, the thought of ever fishing there again still cows me somewhat.

Overhanging willows and remains of the old grist
mill made the Union Street Dam area beautiful.

THE UNION STREET DAM

THE SWIFT WATER below the Union Street Dam is still a good place to fish but it can't begin to compare in beauty with what was there in the 1930s.

Modern-day anglers who never saw the old dam area can't imagine the comparison between old and new as they try for steelhead and Pacific salmon below the concrete dam and its nearby fish ladder.

The old dam was mostly of earth construction with just enough concrete buried inside to make it safe for those early days. Boards to control the flow of water and keep the level of Boardman Lake regular were raised and lowered by hand.

Water coming over the dam entered a long, wooden flume that had once extended nearly to the present Union Street Bridge. By the 1930s, though, much of it had disappeared but enough still remained to shoot quite a volume of white water downstream into the Boardman River.

The entire area was surrounded by enormous willow trees which thrived in that wet environment. Just to the south there were the fieldstone arches, all that was left of what had once been the pioneer Hannah & Lay Mill. When it finally burned, the resulting side shoot became a series of watery steps that served as a rather natural fish ladder.

As a kid, newly arrived in Traverse City in that era, I was fascinated by the fishing opportunities at the Union Street Dam. In fact, it was one of the very first places I went fishing when I saw how many smallmouth bass gathered there.

Opening day of the bass season, in fact, I made it a point to be there at daylight to try for some of those spectacular, fighting fish. Armed with a split bamboo flyrod that I had bought at Montgomery Ward for $1.50, 1 first tried a little silver spinner below which I had fastened on a red hackle fly.

I was able to see several smallmouths swimming on the edge of the swift current. They were apparently intent on spawning.

Maybe it wouldn't have made any difference what kind of lure I had attached to the sturdy leader because such spawners are apt to hit nearly anything that comes close to a bedding area. Anyhow, I was immediately rewarded with a smashing strike.

The bass erupted from the river, shaking its head violently but I managed to keep up a tight line and finally led it into the edge of the stream, then into my waiting landing net. After admiring the muscular body for a few moments and tying it to a stringer, I went back for another try.

Pretty much the same thing happened over and over until I soon had a hefty stringer of smallmouths that gave me my five-fish opening day limit. You can't imagine a prouder kid that I was when I came pedaling my bike back home with that fine catch of smallmouth bass in the basket.

Mom was equally delighted and after I had cleaned the fish she decided they would be the main course for dinner. Dad was delighted, too, when he got home from his day's work at the Grand Traverse Metal Company, just a couple blocks distant.

With my sister, LaVerne, joining us, we really looked forward to that meal of fresh-caught Boardman River bass. All of us dug into the fish with enthusiasm about the same time.

We also paused pretty much together, looking at one another in puzzlement. What was wrong with the taste of these fish?

Most of them went into the garbage can despite our tendency toward not wasting anything in those days when still feeling the effects from the Great Depression.

Determined to solve the mystery, I went back to the Union Street Dam fishing again the next day. This time, though, I walked the whole shoreline on the north side where I had fished the day before. I found more smallmouths willing to be caught but this time I released every one since I couldn't see the sense in keeping fish not fit to be eaten.

Along that bank of the river, I found the probable cause. With downright disgust, I discovered there were several open sewers coming from somewhere up above to the north where a couple old houses were located. It was quite obvious that the toilet paper and everything that went with it was being flushed directly into the Boardman River.

Furious at what I regarded as a violation of health laws, I sat down and wrote a letter to the Traverse City Record-Eagle. It was never published, though, leading me to believe that while such pollution was known, nobody was going to do anything about it.

During the next few years, I continued to fish the Union Street Dam area and found could also catch steelhead trout that also provided sizzling runs and magnificent, head-shaking leaps. After keeping the first one, though, and finding it as tainted in taste as the smallmouths had been, I began releasing every trout, too.

My biggest steelhead were caught on a nightcrawler hooked through the middle and left to dangle in a natural manner. The fish liked to lie in the current of the side water just below the stone archways of the old mill building. One I opened up had its stomach full of little lampreys so the trout were probably mistaking my nightcrawler offerings for those other

139

more-plentiful live foods.

I also soon discovered I could catch the trout on flies when I used nymphs that closely resembled tiny, freshwater shrimp. They provided me with a lot of fun as I laid out a nymph from the southeast base of the Union Street Bridge, worked it slowly after letting it sink down, then waited for the vicious strike. Those were mostly smaller rainbows, although some ran into the three-pound range. The biggest I ever caught that way scaled exactly eight pounds.

At times, as I fought those scrappy trout on my fly tackle, I found the Union Street Bridge lined with amazed spectators. Most were especially startled when, after landing a nice steelhead, I would just measure it for my records, then slip it back into the river.

One woman practically screeched at me when I did that and asked if she could have the next one if I didn't want it. "I guess you don't like their 'green taste, or you wouldn't let them go," was the way she put it. I agreed that I didn't but gave her the next one I caught. She showed up several more evenings when I was fishing and asked for more trout so I guess she didn't mind the taste.

The thought of such blatant pollution really bothered me, though, and I kept making a nuisance at the local Health Department office. They must have finally tired of it and one day one of the workers said I should join him while he took care of the problem.

On our way to the river he said they hadn't been able to find out exactly where the sewage was coming from but he had a solution, anyhow. He sure did. When we got to the place where the sewers emptied into the river below the dam, the water was low enough that he was able to stuff some old cement bags into the four-inch pipes. He followed that up by mixing up some cement and trowled that in, too.

That was the end of the sewage problem below the Union

Street Dam. I never did hear of any complaints from anybody but I'll bet there were a couple of really spectacular toilet backups that couldn't be cured except by hooking up to the regular city sewage system!

Unfortunately, that was not the end of the pollution problem in the Boardman River below the lake. For a number of years, beginning in mid-summer and continuing for weeks, the stream below the Union Street Dam became impossible to fish at all. Each cast made into the stream brought back line and lure draped with a disgusting white slime. If there were fish in the river they were unable to even see a bait under those conditions.

Again, I complained every which way I could, as did most of the other local fishermen. It did no good at all. I remember talking to Claude Kistler at the local Health Department office and telling him it was the cherry canneries that were pouring the slime into the river without sufficient treatment.

Claude, however, denied there was any connection at all and blamed it on "the annual bloom of plants" in Boardman Lake. I nearly gagged on that explanation and continued what was pretty much a futile argument for years.

Eventually, the summer-long slime disappeared from the Boardman River in downtown Traverse City. In a strange "coincidence," it vanished at the same time the last of the cherry canneries were forced to move out of town to new locations. Imagine that!

Today, the modernistic, manicured Union Street Dam still attracts fishermen, most trying to hook one of the steelhead running up out of Grand Traverse Bay. In the fall, activity heats up when a few chinook salmon make it past a new harvest weir just below the Front Street Bridge. Many of the fish not caught by anglers continue up the concrete fish ladder to Boardman Lake or even as far upstream as the Sabin Dam.

Maybe this all furnishes a lot more recreation than was

possible in the "good old days" of the 1930s. But it's a certainty that nobody had more fun in the beautiful surroundings than I did in the willow-draped waters below the old Union Street Dam back then.

A leaky rowboat made it possible to explore an
island south of Boardman lake.

BOARDMAN LAKE WAS PARADISE

IT MAY BE difficult for anyone to visualize now but that area at the south end of Boardman Lake named Logan's Landing was once a really great place to hunt and fish. When I was a kid, back in the 1930s, a school friend, Bob Chamberlain, lived there with his mother and stepfather, the Sybrandts. Their little farmhouse is long gone but there is still a Sybrandt Road remaining in the area which overlooks a stump-filled bay on the lake to the east.

Very often, I would ride my bicycle out there after school or on a Saturday and Bob and I would roam the entire Boardman River valley all the way upstream to Sabin Dam. We felt like a couple of Daniel Boones in hunting and trapping seasons and our frequent success with guns or traps helped to confirm that youthful opinion.

It was all completely wild without a sign of civilization other than the Sybrandt house and barn up on the hill. We hunted for rabbits on the little peninsula on the west side near the rivermouth and often jumped ducks from the stream. Where it entered Boardman Lake, there were two low islands mostly covered with willows. The water between them and the mainland was shallow enough that, by being careful, we could wade with hip boots.

We sometimes did that, quietly enough that we might surprise ducks and coots that were otherwise hidden along the two little islands. Most of the ducks were blacks, big enough to provide a meal for Mom, Dad, my sister and myself, at home. Armed with single-barrel shotguns, Bob and I knew we had to make that first and only shot count. Black ducks were always wary and often jumped and flew before we were in decent range.

The same semi-wet islands usually held jacksnipe, too, but we rarely bothered with them. They flew fast and in crazy, corkscrew fashion on windy days and you could waste a lot of expensive shotgun shells trying to collect enough of them to make worthwhile eating.

Cottontails were something else. We used to walk up a few of the brown rabbits or, when I would bring my little beagle, Buster, along we could count on some exciting shooting. Since the area was rather low and wet on the little peninsula, the bunnies didn't hole up as easily and, given enough time, the dog would circle a rabbit to one of us. (Today, there's a shopping complex right there.)

When it snowed, we could locate regular rabbit runways but failing to find the bunnies then, Bob had another trick. Although it wasn't legal, he would set a heavy cord snare in a runway. By the next morning, he would find it had either been bumped out of the way or, occasionally, it had a thrashing cottontail in the little lasso.

One day we saw a white weasel dart into a hollow log. Probing with a long stick failed to dislodge it, so I set a heavy rat trap there and baited it with a bit of bloody liver. The next day, Bob showed up at school with a paper sack and put in my locker. In it was the dead weasel, killed instantly in my trap.

Weasels, I found out then, have a slightly musky odor and even with the bag rolled shut, I'm sure a few of the nearby locker owners were wondering where that strange smell was coming from. I took it right home after school and managed to skin the weasel and stretch the little glossy-white pelt with its black-tipped tail. I had what is sometimes called an "ermine," one of the most expensive furs. That, though, didn't help me to ever sell my single catch.

Sometimes, when Bob had too many chores to get away, Fred Swaney would join me in roaming the wilds at the south end of Boardman Lake. There were a number of tiny ponds or wet spots along the west side of the river and very often we jumped and shot ducks from them. They included not only the coveted black ducks and an occasional greenhead mallard but such midgets as green-winged and blue-winged teal. If it was edible, we at least tried to shoot whatever was available. Such wild game helped to stretch the meager food budgets we knew our mothers had to work with in those post-Depression days.

Later on in the hunting seasons, the flight ducks came in but mostly they stayed out in Boardman Lake where we couldn't reach them. They were the black and white divers such as bluebills, goldeneyes and buffleheads, for the most part. They helped the home larder, too, when we could manage to shoot one of them.

On the west side of the river and some distance to the south was what we referred to as the "Turtle Pond." It was much larger than the other riverside puddles and it usually held ducks. One day, when I was there alone, I made a rare discovery. On the pond were a half-dozen big Canada geese! Oh, if I could only sneak them close enough to get one, I thought to myself, then went about trying.

Since they hadn't seen me, I flopped on my belly and, shotgun lying across my outstretched arms, began to wriggle gradually in their direction. The closer I got, the more excited I became. It was obvious to me that my strategy might work as I was nearly close enough to get a shot at the sitting geese. Maybe I could even line up two of them and bag a pair!

My dreams of such a feat vanished when a shot rang out from the opposite side of the pond. The geese immediately took wing, still slightly out of range, and flew on up the river. Furious, I jumped up and headed around to where the shot had come from.

That's where I found Fred Swaney, who had come from a different direction and had seen a little bufflehead duck there. He had also sneaked up and got within range before standing up to shoot. And then he missed the butterball!

I was so mad at what happened that I don't think I even spoke to Fred for a week. After that, I finally got sensible and convinced myself that neither of us could have known the other was at the pond so it really was nobody's fault. Fred, of course, apologized all over the place because neither of us had ever come even close to shooting a goose. (Neither of us did that for a number of years.)

The area where Logan's Landing is located now is actually an island, surrounded by the Boardman River to the west and a stump-filled "deadstream" side branch of the river to the east. Completely isolated then, it remained that way for many years until South Airport Road was built across both waterways. It now carries heavy, four-lane traffic every day as the Traverse City area continues to expand its "civilization."

For a kid, though, the idea of an island which couldn't be reached, was something of a lofty challenge. I determined to get over there to see what was on it. I had my kayak but lacking a car to carry it closer, the only alternative would be to carry the craft from East Ninth Street, where I lived, then put it into Boardman Lake and paddle its full length south. By then, though, I would probably be too tired to do much island exploration, much less hunting, too.

Some higher power must look out for kids with such weighty problems. The solution came for me when I found a derelict rowboat one day, sunk in the shallows of Boardman Lake. It was wooden and heavy but somehow I managed to haul it far enough up onto shore to bail it out. After a few days in the sun, I found it would actually float and since nobody showed up to claim it, I figured I had a boat. Admittedly, it was somewhat leaky but regular bailing would take care of that.

Getting oars was something else but I figured that out, too, as there was no other means to propel the clumsy craft. Several long nights of picking nightcrawlers from the lawn of the Asylum grounds gave me 500 of the big worms which I sold to a local bait dealer for a penny apiece.

With that $5 in hand, I did some careful shopping and finally found a pair of used oars, complete with oarlocks, loaded them somehow onto my bicycle and peddled away to the head of Boardman Lake.

The maiden voyage of the new (to me) boat and its "Armstrong" power went great. The craft was heavier than I had realized and leaked quite a little but I was sure it would serve me well. I could hardly wait for the next Saturday to arrive so I could bring Buster along and we would explore the mysterious island. I didn't even mention it to Bob or Fred. This one I deserved to do first and alone.

Current in the Boardman River anywhere is pretty swift and I had worked up a good sweat by the time I had propelled the old rowboat upstream far enough to satisfy me. Finally, though, I began to pull for the far shore and a suitable tie-up spot where I could leave it in water shallow enough that the boat wouldn't sink before I returned.

Buster piled out of the boat as soon as we reached the east river bank and vanished into the brush. It wasn't very long before he was yapping on a hot track which I was positive had to be a cottontail. Finding an opening, I waited patiently and, sure enough, the brown bunny finally came hopping along. I rolled it with my trusty single-shot 16-gauge.

In the days of exploration which followed, I found all kinds of exciting things on what I finally began to call my own private "Paradise Island." After all, how many places has anybody ever found that nobody else knows about but which contains rabbits, ruffed grouse, woodcock and even a few pheasants? Maybe I was selfish with my discovery but I never did tell Fred or Bob or anybody else about my wonderful discovery.

Even today, when I drive along South Airport Road and cross the twin streams near Logan's Landing, I get a twinge of nostalgia. I see a kid and a little beagle in a leaky rowboat struggling across the current enroute to adventure!

Prices for everything in 1939 were almost unbelievable compared to what they are today.

1939 PRICES WERE AMAZING

THE YEAR OF 1939 was an especially big event for 161 of us who lived in Traverse City. June marked graduation from Traverse City High School, then located between West Seventh and Eighth streets. The building was later turned into a grade school but the Lars Hockstad Auditorium is as busy as ever, hosting the Rotary Minstrels, a Kiwanis travel lecture series and other notable events plus, of course, school functions.

What was life really like in 1939, only a few years before the advent of World War II?

For one thing, Traverse City, along with all other communities in the United States, was still in the grip of the Great Depression. The effects of what happened in 1929 hung on into the late 1930s and early 1940s. It was only the start of World War II which really resulted in near-full employment of everybody who wanted to work.

It also was the beginning of price rises that still plague us today. Some of the 1938-39 editions of the Traverse City Record-Eagle provide startling information when measured against things of today. By date, here's the way it was:

Oct. 1, 1938 — Martha Raye was playing at the Lyric Theater in "Give Me A Sailor." Lead football story on the sports page read, "Trojans Take Rugged Gaylord Crew 25-6

In Home Opening." Starting lineup was Rokos, Jack Woodrow, Jim Woodrow, Coates, Gardner, Fifarek, Cavanaugh, Hemming, Loomis, Alward and Langs. In baseball, Hank Greenberg was playing with the Detroit Tigers.

A news story declared: "Prime minister on the spot, forced to defend pact with Nazis." Publisher of the Record-Eagle was Austin Batdorff. Ads included one in which a home on East Ninth Street was for sale. It had eight rooms and a bath; the asking price, $2,200.

Oct. 4 — A new 1939 Packard was advertised for $1,147. The classifieds told of a dance at Karlin every Saturday night, with tickets for gents 25 cents. Franklin Delano Roosevelt was President of the United States. Dizzy Dean was pitching in the World Series for the New York Yankees against the Chicago Cubs.

Oct. 5 — The "Farm & Home" page carried a story: "201 hens die in laying contest." Hamilton's advertised men's suits for $25. Coffee was 35 cents a pound; sirloin steak, 32 cents a pound.

Oct. 27 — The first frost arrived. The new Blue Water Bridge was opened between Port Huron and Sarnia, Ontario. The Yankees swept the Cubs in four straight.

Nov. 8 — Republican candidate Frank G. Fitzgerald won Michigan's highest office from Gov. Frank Murphy. Adolph L. LaFranier elected mayor of Traverse City.

Nov. 9-10 — The Lars Hockstad Auditorium was the site of "Gone With the Wind," a burlesque sponsored by the Kiwanis. The same popular movie was sharing the screens with "Wizard of Oz," "Mr. Smith Goes to Washington" and "Of Mice and Men."

Nov. 11 — "Armistice Day finds U. S. rearming," said a Record-Eagle story.

April 1, 1939 — First dipping of Cold Creek smelt at Beulah tonight. The Coliseum skating rink burned down.

April 4 — Class valedictorian Donald Gilbert and salutatorian Joanne Bauman made the front page. A wave of goldfish swallowing was the latest college campus fad. Robinette Cornell was chosen queen of the National Trout Festival at Kalkaska.

April 8 — Two Benzonia girls won a prize at the Smelt Festival by swallowing live smelt. Mobilgas was selling six gallons of gasoline for $1. A local band was scheduled to play in Detroit, billed from Traverse City as "Cherryland Band." The Elk Tavern opened in Elk Rapids, with free dancing to the "Buddies of Rythym."

April 17 — Baseball celebrated its 100th birthday. John Maxbauer bought the Northern Creamery.

April 26 — The "Yankee Clipper," largest plane to ever fly the Atlantic, arrived in Southampton, England. The flight was preparatory to establishment of regular passenger transatlantic flights.

April 26 — Hitler scorns Roosevelt's "Request for Peace" in a speech to the Reichstag.

Does anybody remember Old Oscar Pepper whiskey? It was known as OOP. Popular dance spots for high school students were the We-Que-Tong Club and O-At-Ka Beach, on both arms of Grand Traverse Bay.

May 1 — There were hints that Thomas E. Dewey might run against Roosevelt in 1940. No nylon pantyhose yet but silk stockings cost 79 cents a pair.

May 12 — "Frost cuts cherry crop 50 percent," said a Record-Eagle farm page story. (Some things never seem to change.)

May 13 —"Frost damage not so serious as first believed." (That hasn't changed, either.) Pepsi-Cola was 5 cents a bottle — and advertised as "Worth a Dime!"

May 30 — Petertyl Drugs advertised free goldfish; the reason not stated in ad.

June 2 — A government survey said Michigan wages were highest in the nation. Average: $1,102 a year.

The Central High School honors assembly was held. The Record-Eagle had a typo. Meaning to say the graduating class "filed" out, it printed the class "fled" out of the auditorium. (Maybe it wasn't really a misprint?)

June 5 — For one day, Central High School outranked wars and rumors of war, on the front page. The banner read: "HIGH SCHOOL WILL END FOR 161 THURSDAY EVE."

For some, it meant going on to college. I had no money for such further education but continued reading everything I could find on the workings of nature, as I still harbored the desire to someday become an outdoor writer. I would, I vowed, one day have my outdoor writings in some newspaper similar to what Ebb Warren did in the Record-Eagle until the management, in the late 1930s, decided the outdoors wasn't very important. (That's when they found how many outraged fishermen and hunters lived in the Grand Traverse region.)

Dad's spirit seemed to be present when fishing
for brook trout years later.

PINCH-HITTING FOR DAD

THEY SAY YOU can't go back. The heck you can't! In cleaning out the garage in 1987, preparatory to moving to a new home in Traverse City, I found something I had nearly forgotten. It was Dad's old rod and reel he had always used for trout fishing.

When we moved, I took it along and with a little better arrangement in the new place, found a place to hang it up alongside of my other variety of fishing tackle. That's where it was when I got to wondering where to spend the first day of the 1988 Michigan trout season on the last Saturday in April.

Remembering how much Dad loved to fish for brook trout, that's what came to mind just about the same time I looked up and saw his old outfit. That was it — I would be a stand-in for Dad on his favorite little creek. It would be just like having him along. Well, sort of, anyhow.

Dad was a wonderful old gentleman who dearly enjoyed "crick fishing," especially when it involved brookies. It was he who taught me my love of the outdoors which has stood me so well all these years.

Among the things I learned from him was how to catch brook trout from creeks, although that took a while, mainly due to my stubborn, kid nature. When I went through the entire first trout season back in 1937 and had caught only 22 trout, it finally sank into my skull that Dad just might know what he-was talking about.

I adopted his method of sneaking up quietly to each trout hole, crawling if necessary to avoid casting a shadow across the creek, and not vibrating the soft ground underlain with springs. It worked! During that next season, my kid records revealed I had caught 149 trout. The year after added over 250 more of the speckled beauties. Finances were pretty tight back then and I was happy to contribute my trout catches to those of Dad for the family larder.

Prior to the trout opener, I examined Dad's old steel telescoping rod with its heavy automatic fly reel attached. I found the same 4-foot leader still in place, with a sharp gold hook that still contained a dried-up worm. Dad always hated to take his worm off the hook until he was sure he wouldn't find one more hole to fish on the way back to our starting point.

That petrified worm had been there since trout season ended in 1979. Dad died that same year in December while sitting at the dining room table addressing Christmas cards to his and Mom's many friends. Up until then, he just didn't seem to have time to ever get sick. All of us should be that lucky!

Daylight on opening morning found me crawling up on his favorite trout stream, a tiny trickle I still refer to as "Dad's Creek." No, I'm not going to say where it is, other than Grand Traverse County.

It was cold, with a thick cover of frost on the ground but doing it like Dad would, I cautiously approached the first pasture pool. I had pulled the steel telescopic rod out to its full length and stripped just enough line off the automatic reel to make sure the old leader would stay clear of the rod guides. The old, dried-up worm had been removed and replaced with a fresh, squirming one.

The little creek had undergone some changes, due to the

years, although all streams continue to change in some respects. Dropping the worm carefully into the current, I let it drift down into the pool. I saw the leader jerk convulsively just before tightening the line and feeling that wonderful, electric throb of a trout taking a bait.

Such fishing involves no finesse at all. In one motion you set the hook and swing the trout out onto the bank. In most cases, this will be accomplished before the fish flops off and tumbles back into the water.

As the first sun's rays caught the trout's arc through the air, within me I thought I heard a voice saying, "Aw, it's only a rainbow!"

That would have been Dad's exact reaction, as anything but a brook trout just wasn't worth a whole lot. This one was a legal 8-incher but I had been thinking brookies so hard I slipped it back into the creek. I could imagine Dad approved of that.

Eventually, other fishermen appeared on the creek banks, invariably stomping along and casting their shadows across the water. They said they hadn't caught anything, which didn't surprise me at all. I continued fishing on upstream, catching a few miniature rainbows and one brown trout as I went but didn't keep any of them.

Dad's Creek has its headwaters in a cedar swamp and it was there, away from the human traffic that I finally found what I was seeking. In one spot I studied a pool that seemed to be impossible to get any kind of bait to without tangling up in overhanging cedar branches. The same strange voice within me, though, kept urging, "You can do it. Try it."

Still with doubts, I swung the worm-baited gold hook in a short looping cast. I was amazed when it went through the only possible opening and drifted toward the shadows.

Although low to the ground, I still saw a dark form dart out from under the tree roots, grab the worm and retreat into the darkness. A quick flip of the steel rod and a 9-inch brook trout landed right at my feet.

"Atta boy, Gord!" the voice enthused. Hey, I was pretty pleased, too!

In short order, I creeled two more brilliantly-marked brookies, resplendent in their jewel-studded bodies and white-rimmed orange fins. Truly, there is no more lovely fish anywhere.

To me, though, they were all the more precious because I had caught them just the way Dad would have. Right then I felt extremely close to him.

A trio of brook trout, caught the old-fashioned way, might not seem like much to today's angler accustomed to trophy steelhead and salmon catches. But to me they proved once again that death is in no way final.

Happy fishing, Dad.

WHATEVER HAPPENED TO... ?

F OR SOME REASON, most books tend to leave you wondering: "Whatever happened to ... ?" Well, this one
won't. Here's a final rundown on our characters:

THE BOY

As was the case with many in my high school class of 1939,
I changed from boy to man somewhere between 1942-45
during World War II. Mostly, I worked in Army radio intel-
ligence, intercepting and sometimes cracking Japanese coded
messages.

That paved the way for me to later work at radio station
WTCM in Traverse City for seven years as a disc jockey,
announcer and news caster. It was a fun job but I wanted to be
a writer and 1952 found me at the Traverse City Record-
Eagle where I soon became outdoor editor, a fulfillment of my
boyhood dream. Imagine fishing and hunting and other
outdoor pastimes and getting paid for doing them!

During one ten-year period, I left the Record-Eagle before
returning to Traverse City and that same position as outdoor

editor. While gone, I served as Chief of Information & Education for the South Dakota Dept. of Game, Fish & Parks and
editor of the "South Dakota Conservation Digest," despite
having no formal college education. Constant reading made
the difference for me. I was enticed back to Michigan to
become editor of the "Michigan Out-of-Doors" magazine in
Lansing before heading back north again.

Travel writing also tied in nicely with outdoor writing and
I managed to seek out stories on six continents for magazines
and newspapers through the years. Amidst all of this activity,
I also found time to turn out three books and have now added
this one.

Dorothy Hahnenberg and I were married in 1947 after I
had often courted her musically with records over WTCM.
She didn't object, either, when I changed my interests from
radio to outdoor and travel writing, for which I thank her
understanding. We have four grown children, two of each,
plus eight grandchildren now, all healthy and happy. Who
could ask for anything more?

THE BIKE

Purchased at a department store in downtown Columbus,
Ohio, this fine steed served me well as transportation up until
the time I decided to enlist in the U. S. Army in 1942. By then,
it had carried me, along with Dad, over many miles around the
Traverse City area on a wonderful number of outdoor adventures — all with only one flat tire! What an amazing product
of manufacturing it was.

By then, of course, Dad had finally bought a car so I was
having less need of a bicycle then. Besides, not knowing just

how long it might take me to win World War II and get back home again (if at all) I reluctantly decided the time had come to let somebody else get use out of my faithful pedal-power companion.

Accordingly, I loaded the bike into the trunk of the car as far as possible and drove to a bicycle shop located on South Union Street. That's when I found second-hand bikes, even those loaded with nostalgia, don't bring very much money.

Extremely reluctant, I finally accepted the $5 offered for it, then drove back home feeling like I had just betrayed my best friend. I just hope some kid bought it and had as much fun peddling it off to dreams like I had when riding that wonderful two-wheeler.

BUSTER

By the time I went off to war, Buster was beginning to turn white with some of his hair, a sign that his age was catching up with him in dog years. Still, he remained pretty frisky and was eager to chase bunnies at the drop of a hint.

The folks had moved to a new home then, just out of Traverse City, where it was still safe to turn Buster loose occasionally so he could run and keep in shape. He did so at every opportunity, although Dad wasn't able to go along as often as I had been doing.

Buster did view his responsibilities seriously, though. While in service, I got a letter from Mom explaining this. She wrote: "The other day when I was letting Buster out, I told him, 'With Gordon gone now, I sure do miss having a good rabbit dinner once in a while.' And, you will never guess what happened. When Buster came back, he was proudly carrying a dead cottontail which was still warm! He had apparently managed somehow to catch and kill it and brought it home for us! I cooked it and it was really delicious."

Even in an isolated area, however, it is never a good idea to let a dog run loose. That fact became apparent one day when Buster returned from an outing with a huge gash on one side of his head. He had apparently been side-swiped by a passing car but somehow managed to not get killed. A veterinarian sewed him up, gave him a shot of some antibiotic and he recovered nicely.

Still, that sort of took its toll on his desire to roam and he never was quite the same. A year or so later, he died, thus ending an era. The boy survived into manhood but the bike and Buster were both gone when I finally returned to Traverse City after the war.

DAD AND MOM

When Otta Kyselka refused to sell the East Ninth Street house to the folks because he was making too much rent money from it at $25 a month, they decided it was time to quit renting and become home owners elsewhere.

They located a 3-bedroom farmhouse on 35 acres on Barney Road. It had a selling price of $1,000. The Bennets, who also attended Central Methodist Church, knowing the folks were reliable people, agreed to sell it for no down-payment. Improvements would serve that purpose plus regular monthly payments.

That was in 1940 and I was around long enough to help Dad rip out the entire insides of the place, install new sheetrock walls and ceilings and run in water for the kitchen and a new bathroom. While maybe not fancy by today's standards, it took care of their needs the rest of their lives.

Being that far out, though, made it necessary for Dad to finally decide he needed a car to get back and forth to his job at the Grand Traverse Metal Casket Company in Traverse City. That's when he purchased a used 1934 Plymouth sedan which had once been used as a taxi, although he didn't know that at the time.

Since Dad didn't know how to drive but I had gained enough experience with my summer of piloting Houdek's ice truck, I became the chauffeur, getting Dad to work and going after him each night. I could see, though, that wasn't going to work forever and insisted he learn to drive, too.

Dad was extremely nervous the day I went along to see that he got his driver's license. He was driving when we approached the Traverse City police station on Cass Street near Milliken's department store then. In his excitement, he mistakenly put his foot on the clutch pedal instead of the brake and ran right into the side of the police station!

It made an awful racket and I expected to see cops come pouring out from every direction. Amazingly, no such thing happened. When Dad finally recovered his composure, we went inside, got his papers filled out and he took the standard driving test which he easily passed. He was still shaking, though, when we got back home.

Dad left the casket company during the war to help in the effort by working at the Parson's Corporation until victory was achieved. He then returned to his former job until the casket company finally went out of business, due to economic factors.

Mom, meanwhile, was very active at Central Methodist Church and when the opportunity arose there, Dad took on the custodian job, remaining until he finally retired. Both of them enjoyed the grandchildren Dorothy and I gave them and, finally, a couple of great-grandchildren.

Dad died in 1978, while Mom lived another three years. Before that, however, wanting to do something special for Traverse City, they sold the majority of their 35 acres, at a nearly give-away price. It became a major part of the Hickory Hills ski area. (Few people ever knew that.)

FRED SWANEY

Fred graduated from Traverse City high school, too, a couple years after I did and shortly found himself also involved in World War II. He ended up in the Air Force and it didn't surprise me a bit when he later told me he used to "have fun buzzing an old sheep herder's shack in Texas, so close the wind must have taken some of the shingles off!" He quit that kind of stuff after coming back to base with a piece of tree branch imbedded in one wing!

He eventually married a Mississippi gal and after the war they returned to Traverse City for a brief try at WTCM while I was still working there. When Fred tired of that, they headed back to Mississippi where he studied law and for a time, was prosecuting attorney at Holly Springs. A demand for new housing after the war prompted him into developing a number of new projects, as well as restoring several antebellum mansions.

Along the way, he made and lost several fortunes, the last on a huge quail hunting preserve in Mississippi, as proof he never lost his love for the outdoors. Living for a time, too, in Minnesota, he became something of a muskie fishing fanatic while maintaining his love for trout and other finny challenges.

When he was a kid, his mother many times yelled at him: "Frederick Earl Swaney, I hope someday you have a bunch of boys just as mean as you are!" Well, he did have six children, three of each, but they were all the best mannered offspring anyone could want. I'm sure he made his mother aware of that, too.

When Fred retired and moved back to the Traverse City area in 1992, he brought along a new wife and two fine English setters left from his quail preserve venture. He was looking forward to ruffed grouse hunting like we had in the "good old days" but if he has found anything close to that, he's forgotten to tell me about it.

Traverse City is still a fine place to live but the changes that have taken place since a couple of kids rode their bicycles to adventure in the 1930s are almost unbelievable. It's said that "progress" is impossible to halt and I guess that's true. I just wish it would slow down a little bit.